Yesterday's Philadelphia

GEORGE WILSON

Yesterday's

PHILADELPHIA

Seemann's Historic Cities Series No. 13

E. A. Seemann Publishing, Inc.
Miami, Florida

Library of Congress Cataloging in Publication Data

Wilson, George, 1923-
     Yesterday's Philadelphia.

     (Seemann's historic cities series ; no. 13)
     1. Philadelphia--History. I. Title.
F158.3.W67   974.8'11   75-2161
ISBN 0-912458-50-X

COPYRIGHT © 1975 by George Wilson
Library of Congress Catalog Card Number: 75-2161
ISBN 0-912458-50-X

Manufactured in the United States of America

To My Father,
J. Wharton Wilson,
and to all the others who worked
in the old Dock Street Market

Contents

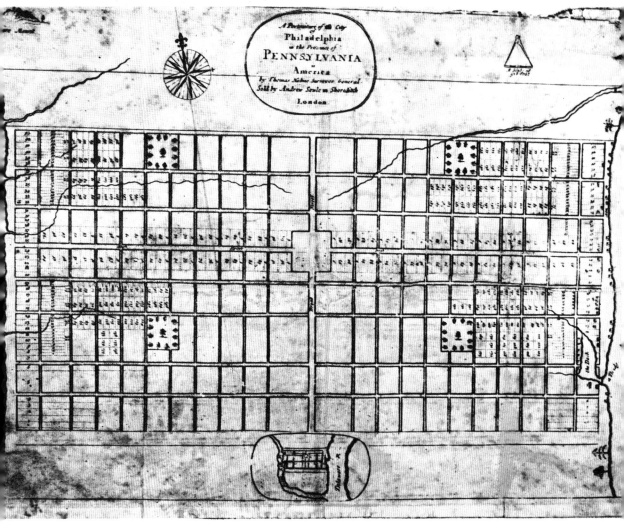

AN EARLY MAP of Philadelphia, used for promotion purposes to attract settlers from Europe, shows the five squares specified by William Penn and laid out by his surveyors. (Inquirer)

Foreword

YESTERDAY'S PHILADELPHIA was many things to many people. To me, it was being born in the front bedroom of a row house on Walnut Street.

It was growing up always knowing when a double-decker bus went by because it would shake the whole house and rattle the dishes in the kitchen cupboard.

It was opening the front door every morning secure in the knowledge that, without fail, there would be two quarts of Supplee milk and a neatly folded copy of *The Philadelphia Inquirer* on the top step.

It was believing that the most fun a small boy could possibly have was to go sailing down the sidewalk on a scooter made out of an old roller-skate, a two-by-four, an orange crate and, if you really wanted to be fancy, a couple of small pieces of wood for handle bars.

It was going to the movies for a dime on Saturday afternoon to be thrilled by cowboy heroes—Buck Jones was my favorite—and never having trouble telling the good guy because he was always the one in the white hat.

It was thinking that the Philadelphia Athletics were the best baseball team in the world, and that Penn was the king of college football—and being right a good part of the time.

It was looking up into the sky, usually in the day but sometimes in the night, and seeing the most awesome sight imaginable: one of those monstrous dirigibles based at Lakehurst, New Jersey, gliding by—ranging from 650 to 785 feet long and, occasionally, flying so low that it seemed you could almost reach up and touch it.

It was going for a joy ride in what everybody then agreed was the most fabulous invention of all time, the automobile, on a quiet street like City Line Avenue, or for real open-road adventure, the Baltimore Pike in Delaware County.

It was having faith, first and foremost, in God and country—and, after that, in the Republican Party and the Pennsylvania Railroad, two all-powerful Philadelphia institutions presumed to be indestructible.

Yesterday's Philadelphia was, of course, far more than these early impressions of one native son. It was a city with a rich heritage of history and culture, of industry and commerce. But it was also a city of people—ordinary people doing the commonplace things of their lives and times.

This book strives for a broad sampling of both the momentous and the routine. It seeks to recapture the way we were—both as a city and as a people. For non-Philadelphians and new Philadelphians, the aim is to be informative as well as entertaining. For old Philadelphians there will be a touch of nostalgia, too.

No one knows more than I how much did not get into this volume. I examined an estimated 45,000 old photographs and drawings, most of them interesting and many of them significant, to select a few hundred. Philadelphia was, and is, one of the great cities of the world. A definitive history is beyond the scope of this work. It presents, for the most part, pictures heretofore unpublished in any history book. Some of them may be faded or less professional appearing than in modern days—it would have been a pity to leave the important ones out just because time has been unkind to the available copies.

Most of the pictures were obtained from the library of *The Philadelphia Inquirer* (credited as "Inquirer") and the Print and Picture Department of the Free Library of Philadelphia ("Free Library"). I acknowledge with gratitude and thanks the valuable guidance and assistance given to me by Frank G. Gradel and Gene V. Loielo of *The Inquirer* library staff, and Robert F. Looney and Diane Welch of the Free Library staff.

George Wilson

Philadelphia, Spring 1975

The First Two Centuries: 1682 to 1882

WILLIAM PENN had a dream and he called it Philadelphia, meaning Brotherly Love. It would be a city where people could live in peace and harmony and happiness. They could worship as they pleased, practicing their religion openly and adhering to their beliefs without risk of ridicule or persecution. Their "green countrie towne" would be beside a beautiful river providing safe harbor for vessels from all over the world. The climate would be moderate, not too hot and not too cold but just right—well, most of the time anyway. And this City of Brotherly Love would be a planned city—one that would not simply grow at random but would have organized growth with streets laid out in orderly fashion and space set aside in advance for public squares where the citizenry could enjoy oases of outdoor greenery within easy walking distance of their homes.

It was not a dream in the conventional meaning. William Penn did not have this vision thrust upon him in an interlude of sleep. It was, rather, a dream in the sense of a glorious goal that he was determined to strive for with all his energy and resources. He wanted to build not just another city but a superb city—a city in which its inhabitants could prosper, a city that they could be proud of, a city that would be a sparkling jewel in the new land across the sea and a city that, above all, would provide sanctuary for the oppressed.

To fail to understand the foregoing is to lack understanding of what Philadelphia is all about. Yesterday's Philadelphia was the embodiment of William Penn's spirit—the successes, the failures, and the frustrations in the pursuit of his ideals. Today's Philadelphia is a city that has come a long way toward measuring up to his expectations. Tomorrow's hope is for a city that will.

Penn was a Quaker. To be a Quaker was considered akin to heresy by some

WHEN WILLIAM PENN arrived in Philadelphia for the first time in October of 1682, his first place of residence was the city's first tavern, The Blue Anchor. Shown here as it appeared about 1700, the tavern was on the west side of Front Street and on the shore of Dock Creek. Penn had a taste for good food, good drink, and good fellowship—as did most early Philadelphians, and later ones also. By 1744 there were more than a hundred taverns in Philadelphia. (Free Library)

in high authority in seventeenth-century England. He was imprisoned for refusing to renounce his religious beliefs. Yet he continued to espouse them—not only in England but on the European continent. He was especially well-known to peoples of Germanic origin, including those belonging to religious sects requiring adherents to be plain in dress and manner. This accounted to some degree for the large number of Germans who were early arrivals in Philadelphia and the many Mennonites, Amish, and Dunkards who settled in rural areas of Pennsylvania. Religious freedom, complete tolerance, and respect for differences in religious customs were the keystone of Penn's grand design for his city and his province.

As the son of a wealthy Englishman, and by inheritance a man of considerable financial substance in his own right, William Penn requested and received from King Charles II in 1680 a tract bordering on the Delaware River in repayment of a loan Penn's father had made to the royal family. Thus

UNDER THIS ELM on the shore of the Delaware River, in what is now the Kensington section of Philadelphia, William Penn signed his famous treaty with the Lenni-Lenape Indians, also known as the Delawares, in 1683. This drawing, about 1710, shows a mansion that was built near the tree in 1702, which was later called the Governor's House because two governors of Pennsylvania during the pre-Revolutionary War period lived there. When the tree was blown down during a storm in 1810, the growth rings disclosed it was 283 years old. The mansion was razed in 1825. (Free Library)

[12]

Pennsylvania, meaning Penn's Woods, was born. He had never been to America, but had received first-hand reports from others who had.

William Markham, named deputy governor of the province by Penn, arrived in 1681 and selected the site for Philadelphia. It was approximately one hundred miles from the entrance to Delaware Bay and fifty miles from the mouth of the Delaware River. The mouth of Dock Creek, near Spruce Street, was chosen as the center of the harbor area. The original boundaries of the city were the Delaware River on the east, the Schuylkill on the west, Vine Street on the north, and South Street on the south. Distances were about two miles from river to river, and one mile from Vine to South.

Penn planned the city in a grid pattern with streets spaced far apart so that houses could have substantial garden areas. The plan fell quickly apart, however, with rapid early growth of the city, an intense demand for housing, and soaring land prices. Large city blocks were divided into small blocks by running streets or alleys through them. The result was far more building lots per original block than Penn had anticipated.

Penn's plan for public squares fared better. He laid out five: Northeast, Southeast, Southwest, Northwest, and Center. The first four have survived as public parks and are now named Franklin, Washington, Rittenhouse, and Logan squares—although the latter used to be the site of public hangings and now contains a traffic circle and a below-ground-level expressway. Center Square is occupied by City Hall but retains remnants of a public square in its open courtyard.

Advance work parties arrived in Philadelphia in late 1681 and early 1682 to begin building the city before Penn's arrival in October of that year on a ship named *Welcome*. Prior to departure from England he had begun promotion of his province with publication of a pamphlet entitled "Information and Direction to Such Persons As Are Inclined to America." Penn was not the high-pressure type of real estate salesman. His pamphlet advised prospective settlers to "be moderate in expectation" and to "count on labour before a crop, and cost before gain." That's still good advice.

The date of Philadelphia's founding is generally recognized as 1682, the year William Penn landed at the mouth of Dock Creek. But neither he nor his advance parties were the first inhabitants. The Lenni-Lenape Indians, later called the Delawares, had lived for a long time, perhaps centuries, in the area that was to become Philadelphia. It was good hunting ground, covered with forests and laced with streams. Some small Indian villages were located within the present city limits at the time of Penn's arrival. The Indian name for the land between the two rivers—the Delaware and the Schuylkill—was Coaquannock, meaning Grove of Tall Pines.

Englishman Henry Hudson, sailing under the Dutch flag, entered Delaware Bay in 1609 and is credited with its discovery, although several earlier European explorers may have sighted the mouth of the bay. In 1610 Englishman

THE FIRST PUBLIC SCHOOL in Philadelphia, seen on the right in this sketch made in the early 1700s, opened in 1689 on the east side of Fourth Street south of Chestnut. The building on the left was the Friend's Meeting House. Operated by the Society of Friends, the school charged tuition for children whose parents or guardians could afford to pay, but was free for others. This was the forerunner of the William Penn Charter School, subsequently relocated in the East Falls section of Philadelphia. An earlier school, the city's first, had been established in 1683, but enrollment was restricted to tuition-paying pupils. In that same year, the Pennsylvania Assembly enacted a compulsory education law requiring all parents and guardians to teach or have someone else teach their children to read and write by the age of twelve. (Free Library)

WILLIAM PENN was about fifty years old when this portrait was made in the 1690s. The original is in the collection of the Historical Society of Pennsylvania. (Inquirer)

[14]

WILLIAM PENN'S Slate Roof House, so named because it was the first building in the American colonies to have such a roof, is depicted in this old drawing as it appeared in 1698. It was on the east side of Second Street north of Walnut, at the corner of Norris Alley. When Penn returned to Philadelphia from England after an absence of fifteen years in December of 1699, with his second wife, Hannah, the house awaited them. John Penn, their son, was born here on January 29, 1700. The substantial dwelling stood for more than a century before being demolished in the 1860s, one of the many instances in which Philadelphians of the past have shown shocking disregard for historic landmarks. (Free Library)

Samuel Argall, en route to Virginia, sailed into the bay and named it in honor of Lord de la Warr, then governor of Virginia. But it was a Dutch sea captain, Cornelis Hendricksen, who in 1616 became the first European to sail up the Delaware River as far as the future site of Philadelphia. He went ashore near the mouth of the Schuylkill, making peaceful and friendly contact with the Indians.

The Dutch were the first settlers in what is now Philadelphia, starting a colony on the east bank of the Schuylkill in 1633. The Swedes settled in the early 1640s in what is now Delaware County, south of Philadelphia, and by the 1660s were firmly established along the shore of the Delaware in what is presently the Southwark section of South Philadelphia. There was also a Swedish settlement a few miles upstream in what has become the Tacony section of Northeast Philadelphia.

These settlements were frontier outposts, nothing more. Within the boundaries of today's Philadelphia there were only a few hundred European colonists when Penn's first advance party arrived. And virtually none of them lived within the original borders of Penn's city, although the Southwark Swedes were next-door neighbors.

It was when William Penn hit town that things began to happen—and fast. Within two years, by 1684, the city had 300 houses and 2,500 inhabitants. It had a variety of shops and stores, a school and, yes, even a jail. A municipal government had been established, and a court system. From late spring to early fall new settlers from Europe were arriving at the rate of a shipload a week. Many of them were skilled people: carpenters, bricklayers, tailors, weavers, cobblers, and brewers—to mention just a few of the trades represented in the early years. Meanwhile, with Penn's approval and encouragement, a group of ten settlers headed by Francis Daniel Pastorius had founded Germantown in 1683. It quickly organized a local government of its own and was a separate municipality for more than a century and a half before becoming a part of Philadelphia.

Penn made a point of contacting the Indians early, meeting with them on their home grounds and establishing friendly relations on an informal basis as well as through formal negotiation of a treaty of friendship. Thus there was peace along with the prosperity as Philadelphia became an instant boom town. The amenities of seventeenth-century civilization, such as they were, replaced the wilderness with remarkable swiftness. The city had been literally chopped and hacked out of the forest. Yet within just a few years people were living comfortably in brick homes amply furnished with imports from England. Although Philadelphia was but a speck on the edge of a vast and unexplored panorama of woods and wild animals and no one knew what else, the inhabitants of the city were not frontiersmen in the traditional sense. The urban way of life, as reflected in dress and manners, was transplanted intact from England to the shore of the Delaware. Instead of trying to get away from it all, Philadelphians for the most part simply brought it with them.

This is not to suggest that life was easy in earliest Philadelphia. For many it was hard, and for some it was cruel.

Just getting to Philadelphia was an ordeal. Accommodations aboard ship ranged from crowded to overcrowded. If you were exceptionally fortunate, the trip across the ocean could be made in a month. If the weather was bad or the captain managed to get lost—or both, as often happened—the voyage could take as long as four months. Most ships made it in six to nine weeks.

Many passengers lacked the money to pay their fare. They sailed under a system of voluntary white slavery known as indentured servitude. When the ship arrived in Philadelphia, the captain sold the services of the non-payers for a stipulated period of time, usually four or five years, to persons who were willing to buy the service by paying the fare. In an era when credit cards had not yet been invented, this sail-now-pay-later plan worked reasonably well. The sea captain got his money, the buyer of the indentured servant obtained cheap if not always diligent labor, and the penniless traveler not only got to where he wanted to go but also had instant long-term employment with room and board provided.

Black slavery was much worse. It was involuntary and usually permanent, although some persons bought slaves and set them free. The paradox of slavery in the City of Brotherly Love is hard to explain and impossible to justify. Slave auctions were held in the city and also aboard ships in the harbor that had brought black captives from Africa. Some slave owners attempted to rationalize their position by insisting that their slaves were well-fed, well-clothed, and well-treated. Some were. John Bartram, Philadelphia's distinguished botanist, was proud of the fact that he, his wife, and his children ate at the same table with his slaves. Nonetheless, there were many in early Philadelphia who knew that slavery was inhuman and inexcusable and said so. The first petition in America for the abolition of slavery originated in Germantown in 1688. The Society of Friends in Philadelphia called for abolition in 1696.

Meanwhile, though, things were going from bad to worse for the slaves. Because Sunday was a day of rest for many of them, as for their owners, the presence of idle slaves on the streets of the city on the Sabbath was deemed a problem. Beginning in 1693 any slave caught on a city street on Sunday not accompanied by the owner, or with written permission of the owner to be on the street, was subject to immediate arrest, overnight imprisonment without food or water, and 39 lashes Monday morning. The owner was required to pay the fee charged by the whipper for his services. At least there were no whippings on Sundays. Pious Philadelphians, right from the beginning, took pride in their Sunday Blue Laws.

The stocks, the pillory, and the whipping post were at Second and Market

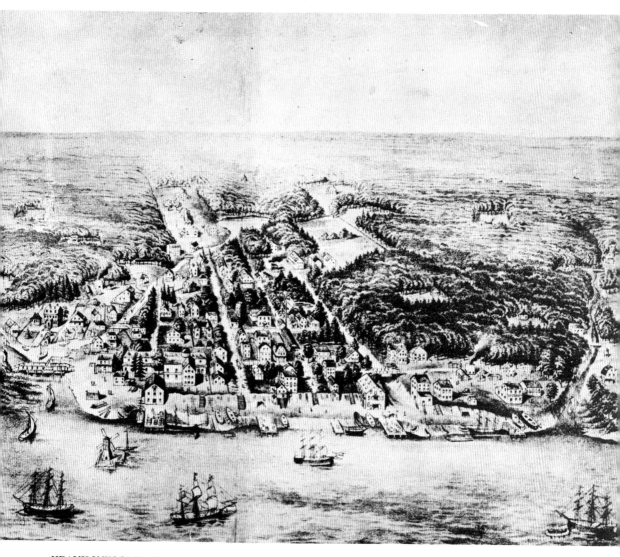

HEAVILY WOODED WILDERNESS still surrounded Philadelphia twenty years after its founding. Although this imaginative 1702 drawing may not be accurate in all details relative to streets and buildings, it dramatizes the ruggedness of the forests that hemmed in the town huddled on the bank of the Delaware. It would have been a long walk through the woods to reach what is now Broad Street. Two caves are visible on the river bank. Many early arrivals in Philadelphia lived in caves until houses could be built. The covered market place can be seen in the middle of Market Street, originally called High Street. That's Chestnut Street extending up from the river in the center of the picture. (Free Library)

BENJAMIN FRANKLIN was sixty-one at the time of this portrait in 1767. The original is in the White House, a gift of Mr. and Mrs. Walter Annenberg of Philadelphia. (Inquirer)

streets so they could be seen by shoppers at the market there. Persons sentenced to stand in the pillory sometimes were additionally sentenced to have their ears nailed to it during the period of confinement. Occasionally, persons sentenced to be whipped were carted about the city, receiving lashes in instalments at various locations so more of the citizenry could witness the punishment without the inconvenience of walking to the public market.

Making public spectacles of human suffering was common practice in America and Europe in those times. In this regard Philadelphia was no worse than other cities, and not as bad as some. No witches were burned in Philadelphia. People were not imprisoned because of their religious beliefs.

William Penn, who was thirty-eight years old when he first arrived in Philadelphia, spent only four years in the city—two visits of two years each. His absence was by necessity, not choice. He was kept busy in England defending his infant city and province against political and religious opponents who sought to deprive him of his land grant. He was charged with treason twice, and acquitted twice.

In 1723, five years after Penn died in England at the age of seventy-four, Benjamin Franklin arrived in Philadelphia as a seventeen-year-old. He became the greatest Philadelphian of all time although he, too, spent much of his life away from the city. Besides living his first 17 years in his native Boston, he was in England for three periods totaling 18 years, and in France for nine years. He lived 84 years and spent 40 of them in Philadelphia. Most of his time abroad was devoted to diplomacy, first in striving to protect the American colonies against English tyranny, and then in obtaining the crucial aid of France in their struggle for independence.

At the age of twenty-three, Franklin was editor and publisher of the *Pennsylvania Gazette* and made the newspaper a powerful voice for civic improvement. At twenty-seven, he began publication of *Poor Richard's Almanack,* which firmly established his reputation as a man with a delightful sense of humor capable of dispensing practical advice on any subject and possessing a wide range of intellectual interests, most notably in science and philosophy.

Franklin was an activist as well as a thinker, providing the initiative and energy and leadership for many of Philadelphia's famous firsts, among them the world's first subscription library, the world's first volunteer fire company, America's first hospital, and America's first fire insurance company. He founded the University of Pennsylvania. He pioneered in the paving and lighting of streets. He published the first textbook and the first novel in America. He founded the American Philosophical Society. His inventions were as varied as they were practical—as, for example, the Franklin stove, bifocal glasses, and the lightning rod. His courageous kite-and-key experiments with lightning gave mankind its first glimpse of a new energy source, electricity, that would revolutionize the world more than a century after his death. He was a leader in the movement to abolish slavery. And he provided both leadership and inspiration in the debates and decisions at Independence Hall in 1776 and 1787 when the Declaration of Independence and the Constitution of the United States were adopted.

Benjamin Franklin died in 1790, the year that Philadelphia became the capital of the United States. The city had grown from 10,000 inhabitants   [19]

TUN TAVERN, near the waterfront south of Chestnut Street, was the birthplace of the United States Marines. This is how it looked about 1780. It became the first official recruiting headquarters for Marines in 1775—one year before the Declaration of Independence.
(Inquirer)

AMERICAN INDEPENDENCE was born on the Fourth of July in 1776 at Independence Hall with formal adoption of the Declaration of Independence by the Second Continental Congress, although the decisive vote to declare independence had been taken two days earlier. The signing of the Declaration, depicted here in a painting by John Trumbull, was on August 2. The painting is in the Capitol in Washington. (Inquirer)

[20]

INDEPENDENCE HALL looked like this in 1776. The wooden sheds at each end provided primitive shelter for visiting Indians. By 1790, when Philadelphia became the capital of the United States for ten years, the sheds had been replaced by a County Court House on the right, and a City Hall on the left. The U. S. Congress convened in the Court House, and the U. S. Supreme Court conducted its business in the City Hall. Note that there was no clock in the tower, but the tower was rebuilt, with a clock, in 1828. (Free Library)

when he arrived in 1723 to 28,000. Philadelphia was the largest city in the country, a distinction it would hold for another forty years before being passed by New York. In 1776, Philadelphia was the second-largest city in the British Empire. London was first. In 1790, the population of Philadelphia County, comprising the present boundaries of the city, was 54,000.

Philadelphia's entire Colonial period thus was marked by steady growth both within the city and in its environs. It emerged as a major seaport despite troublesome pirate activity near the mouth of Delaware Bay in the early 1700s. A new city charter devised by William Penn and adopted in 1701 provided reasonably effective city government. Under Franklin's constant prodding, the city even had clean streets for a while. Vehicular traffic became a problem as the city grew, requiring drastic action in 1768 when chains were placed across Market and Second streets near the market place to keep vehicles out of the area while the markets were open. It was Philadelphia's first pedestrian mall.

Until 1704, volunteers took turns serving as a solitary night watchman who strolled through the city ringing a bell, announcing the time and the weather, and keeping on the lookout for fires. As the result of a growing city and a shrinking supply of volunteers a form of draft was instituted in 1704. The city was divided into ten districts for night watchman purposes, and each citizen was required to take his turn on the streets of his neighborhood or provide a substitute. This system was replaced by paid watchmen on the city payroll in 1758.

Theatrical productions were considered to be of questionable moral value by some of Philadelphia's officials in Colonial times. As a result, America's first theater, the Southwark, opened in 1766 on the south side of South Street west of Fourth, just outside the city limits. The official attitude toward theaters changed quickly, however, when George Washington arrived in the city as President of the United States. He liked the theater and soon was attending a brand-new one, the Chestnut Street Theater, built on the northwest corner of Sixth and Chestnut, diagonally across from the U. S. Capitol.

Philadelphia was blessed with abundant water from earliest times, but problems soon developed. It was customary for settlers who dug wells to share water with new arrivals at no cost. Some people, recognizing a good deal when they saw it, didn't bother to dig wells of their own and just kept using the water of their neighbors. An ordinance in 1713 permitted well owners to charge for water. In 1756, the city began acquiring wells and making water available to the public without charge.

Smoking in the streets of Philadelphia was prohibited by law early in the 1700s—to prevent fire, not air pollution. Every building, including private residences, had to have at least four buckets filled with water, ready for use in case of fire. The city had no fire engines until 1718, when it acquired a hand-drawn one from England. It was in the same year that the city began

PHILADELPHIA's "WHITE HOUSE" is shown here, on the left, as it appeared in 1790 when President and Mrs. George Washington moved in. John Adams and Mrs. Adams also lived here when he was President. Robert Morris, who owned both houses in this picture, lived in the one on the right—at the southeast corner of Sixth and Market streets. The home of the first two U. S. Presidents really wasn't white—it was red brick, and it was called the Executive Mansion. Ironically, British General William Howe had lived in the house during the British occupation of Philadelphia while Washington and his army were at Valley Forge. The house was damaged by fire in 1780 and rebuilt in 1785. (Free Library)

weekly collection of trash and ashes, for fire prevention as much as for cleanliness.

Philadelphia's first public transportation service to New York was inaugurated in 1706. The trip started with a sailboat ride up the river to Burlington, New Jersey, where passengers took a stage coach to Perth Amboy and then another ferry to New York. It was hardly worth the effort, though. There wasn't much to do in New York in those days.

In the last quarter of the eighteenth century, Philadelphia reached its zenith as the focal point of national political power. With the Continental Congresses, the Constitutional Convention, and then the Government of the United States based in Philadelphia, the eyes of Europe as well as America were on William Penn's city as it concluded its first century and commenced its second. Philadelphia also continued as the capital of Pennsylvania through this period—until 1799, when Lancaster became the seat of state government.

Social life reached a high mark during this time also. Members of the Continental Congresses, despite the grim seriousness of the business at hand, were ready for a party or a dance at the drop of an invitation. The same could be said of members of the early U. S. Congresses. George and Martha Washington were good party givers, and their home just a block from the Capitol was the scene of numerous affairs ranging from elaborate state dinners to simpler but still rather formal evenings of eating and drinking and entertainment. The second-floor room that extends across the entire front of Independence Hall was the scene of many banquets and dances, although descending the long staircase afterwards was a stern test for those who had consumed strong drink in generous quantities. There were some nasty falls, including one in which an early governor of Pennsylvania broke both legs. He insisted that he had tripped over his sword.

The decade of the 1790s, when Philadelphia was the national capital, was marred by two yellow fever epidemics—the worst in 1793 when virtually all public business as well as social life came to a halt. Four thousand people died of the fever in Philadelphia that year, including many grave diggers attempting to bury the dead. Bodies littered the streets and lay abandoned in homes. There was a plague of lawlessness also, with thieves stripping bodies of valuables and plundering homes where the residents had died or fled. There was grim retribution for some of the robbers, who also died of the fever. Thousands of inhabitants left the city, including the Washingtons. They spent the summers of 1793 and 1794 at the Deshler-Morris House in Germantown—the same house that British General William Howe had occupied as his headquarters after the retreat of Washington's army in the Battle of Germantown.

Epidemics were tragically common occurrences in eighteenth-century Philadelphia. There had been many previous outbreaks of yellow fever, including three in the 1740s. Smallpox and diphtheria epidemics also had struck the city.

[23]

THE CONSTITUTION of the United States of America was adopted on September 17, 1787, in the same room of Independence Hall where the Declaration of Independence had been approved eleven years earlier. The historic moment in 1787 is depicted in a painting by John H. Froelich whose original is in the Pennsylvania State Museum in Harrisburg. (Inquirer)

THE FIRST U. S. MINT began production in 1792 on the east side of Seventh Street north of Market. Uncirculated coins were stored in vaults in the front building. The coins were made in the middle building, which also contained vaults for the storage of bullion. Smelting and refining were done in the rear building. This mint was in operation until 1832. Every coin made here that is still in existence has gained tremendously in value because of the popularity of coin collecting as a hobby and investment. (Free Library)

But life went on for the survivors of these periodic visitations of diseases. Indeed, it was during the terrible 1740s that the first four months of the year became firmly established as the principal social season. Although partying and dancing were never really out of season, and were enjoyed the year around, winter and early spring were the busiest times on the social calendar, especially for the most elaborate balls. By the mid-1700s, ballrooms were becoming a fixture in homes built by wealthy Philadelphians. And they enjoyed them while they could—before the arrival of hot weather that brought not only discomfort but a perennial threat of epidemics.

Some regular social events were suspended during the Revolutionary War but for many it was business and fun as usual. Parties, bigger and better than ever, marked the ten months of occupation by the British army. Philadelphians loyal to the Crown, numerous until the tide of battle turned, went out of their way to entertain the troops while, twenty miles away at Valley Forge, Washington's men were dying daily in the snow.

It is something that Washington, when he was President, must have thought about as he attended parties in Philadelphia with guest lists that included persons who had entertained the enemy during his bleakest winter.

When President Washington wasn't entertaining or going to parties or attending to affairs of state, he often was seen taking rides through the streets of Philadelphia in a carriage drawn by six horses. During his presidency he had more horses than servants—14 and 10, respectively. Although cobblestones could be rough in places, riding around in the city had become fairly comfortable by the 1790s, thanks in large measure to the street-paving program that had been initiated decades earlier at the insistence of Benjamin Franklin.

Racial injustice prevailed in Philadelphia while it was the U. S. capital, but progress had been made. In 1770, the Society of Friends founded a school for blacks. Although separate and unequal education, it was an enlightened move at a time when slavery was still legal in Pennsylvania and was on the increase in many of the American colonies. In 1790, ten years after slavery had been abolished in Pennsylvania, the entire County of Philadelphia had fewer than 2,500 black inhabitants, about 4.6 percent of the population.

As the nineteenth century began, there were many farewell parties as the U. S. government prepared to move to Washington. But there was one notable absentee, Robert Morris, who had given vast amounts of money to finance the American Revolution in its darkest days when many had written off independence as a lost cause. It was Morris who had provided a home for presidents of the United States and had been the next-door neighbor of Washington and Adams. But Morris missed the goodby parties because he had fallen on hard times, was unable to pay his debts, and, from 1798 to 1801, was confined to the debtors' section of the prison on Walnut Street, one block from the Capitol of the United States. In an era of many strange twists and turns of history, it was the supreme irony.

[25]

JOHN FITCH'S STEAMBOAT, propelled by twelve oars, should have made history on the Delaware River in July of 1786 when it made the first successful trial runs of a steam-driven vessel—but Philadelphians watched more in amusement than amazement, and the world took no notice. On a one-mile test, the craft had an average speed of eight miles per hour. Fitch experimented with both oar and paddle-wheel steamboats between 1785 and 1790 and was successful with both types even though early tests on the Schuylkill were failures. In 1790, Fitch inaugurated regular passenger and freight service between Philadelphia and Trenton, New Jersey, a distance of thirty-three miles, with a sternwheeler that averaged seven to eight miles per hour. Fitch obtained a patent in 1791 and his venture was showing signs of commercial success when he went broke trying to finance construction of a second boat. He died penniless in 1798, a man ahead of his time. In 1807, Robert Fulton unveiled the *Clermont* on the Hudson River, New Yorkers wildly applauded its six-miles-per-hour performance, and he was acclaimed as the inventor of the steamboat. (Inquirer)

THE FIRST BALLOON ASCENSION in America was on January 9, 1793, from the prison yard at Sixth and Walnut streets, south of Independence Square. Jean Pierre Blanchard, a Frenchman, rose to an altitude of more than a mile in the basket beneath the balloon filled with hydrogen. He landed 15 miles away, in Gloucester County, New Jersey, 46 minutes after lift-off. Rush-hour motorists can't make that kind of time today. President Washington was among the spectators and can be seen standing in the center of the three persons at the left. (Inquirer)

PENNSYLVANIA HOSPITAL, shown here at it appeared in the early 1800s, is America's first hospital. Established in 1751, with Benjamin Franklin as the principal founder, it was admitting patients in temporary quarters on Market Street the following year. The cornerstone was laid in 1755 for the hospital's first building at its permanent site between Pine and Spruce streets west of Eighth. The original structure along with many others is still in use. (Free Library)

Having suffered a double loss of political status, with both the state and the nation moving their capitals out of the city in successive years, Philadelphia turned its attention in the 1800s to development of commerce and industry with unprecedented vigor. And there was a leader ready to show the way: Stephen Girard.

Born in France, Girard came to Philadelphia in 1776 at the age of twenty-six, already a successful sea captain and ship owner. He became a one-man conglomerate, making numerous investments in a myriad of business enterprises, including shipping and shipbuilding. Girard-built ships were still sailing in the 1890s. He was a prime mover and shaker in the development of the port of Philadelphia. He was the hero of the yellow fever epidemics in the 1790s—not only by contributing relief funds but also by personally organizing and directing emergency care facilities for the sick. During the War of 1812, he bailed out the U. S. Government when it was in desperate financial trouble and was having difficulty finding buyers for a bond issue. He put a cool five million dollars on the line, confident that the United States of America was the best investment on earth. He was the country's first multi-millionaire. And he was the richest man in America when he died in 1831, worth about $8 million. He died in a rather unusual way for an eighty-one-year-old business tycoon. He was run over by a horse and wagon while trying to cross the street, thus becoming one of Philadelphia's early traffic fatalities.

Girard died a childless widower—his wife had been insane for 25 years before her death—and he left virtually his entire fortune to the City of Philadelphia to be used for a remarkably varied list of specific benefactions—including tax relief, waterfront beautification, improvement of the police force, and the education of "poor, white, male orphans." Girard College—actually an elementary and high school despite its name—was founded to perform the educational function. Disgruntled relatives, cut off without a penny, fought a ferocious battle to break the will. They engaged Daniel Webster as their lawyer. After thirteen years, the will was upheld by the U. S. Supreme Court in a decision that would have pleased Stephen Girard immensely. He was a man who loved a good fight—all the more so if he won.

But the Girard story may never end. His will seems destined to be forever

[27]

STEPHEN GIRARD is shown here in the early nineteenth century. He had lost an eye before coming to Philadelphia, but it did not diminish his perception of the city's great potential as a seaport. (Inquirer)

in litigation. The U. S. Supreme Court, 137 years after Girard's death, declared a part of his will pertaining to Girard College unconstitutional on grounds of racial discrimination.

A year after Girard died, the age of the iron horse was born in Philadelphia. For the next hundred years, railroads were the driving force behind the city's industrial growth. Where tracks went, factories were built—a great variety of manufacturing establishments that provided jobs for immigrants pouring in from Europe. By 1850, the population had reached 121,000 in the city and 408,000 in the county. In 1854, the city population soared almost to the half-million mark as city limits were extended to cover the entire county. Twenty-eight municipalities were consolidated with Philadelphia at one stroke to create the city boundaries that have not changed since.

By 1882, the two-hundredth anniversary of the city's founding, William Penn's "green countrie towne" had become an industrial giant of more than 850,000 inhabitants. But its greatest growth was yet to come.

THE FOURTH OF JULY in 1819 was a festive occasion in Center Square, as depicted in this old print. The square, where City Hall stands now, was a popular place for picnicking, leisurely strolls, and civic celebrations early in the nineteenth century as the city developed westward toward Broad Street. The building in the background, erected in 1801, housed a 16,000-gallon water tank and was part of the municipal water system. The water was pumped from the waterworks which, although no longer in use, still adorns the east bank of the Schuylkill near the Art Museum. (Inquirer)

[28]

TWO VIEWS from the steeple of Independence Hall in 1838 depict a growing city. The view to the east *(above)* shows the City Hall building in left foreground. The steeple of Christ Church (far left) continued to dominate the skyline. Beyond the Delaware River was a still rather rural New Jersey with the city of Camden in the early stages of development. Looking west *(below)*, the County Court House is in the foreground. The city had expanded beyond Broad Street. (Inquirer)

MIKVEH ISRAEL, the first Jewish congregation in Philadelphia, was founded in 1740. Its synagogue at Third and Cherry streets is shown here as it appeared about 1825. (Inquirer)

MARKETS in the middle of Market Street were the focal point of retail business activity, not only in the eighteenth century but through the first half of the nineteenth. This drawing, about 1838, shows the markets extending west from the intersection of Front and Market. Watchboxes on the corners, left and right, provided shelter for policemen in cold or stormy weather while enabling them to keep an eye on activities in all directions. (Inquirer)

CHRIST CHURCH, shown in an 1829 engraving, was built in 1727 and several subsequent years on the west side of Second Street north of Market and has endured as a prime example of Colonial architecture. Its steeple, when completed and equipped with eight chiming bells in 1754, became a Philadelphia landmark in both sight and sound. Worshipers at Episcopal services here included George Washington, Benjamin Franklin, Robert Morris, and Betsy Ross. Lotteries, under Franklin's direction, raised funds for completion of the church. (Free Library)

NO SLUMS are to be seen in this 1839 view of Broad Street looking north from a point about fifty yards north of Girard Avenue. Just 125 years later the area in the left of this picture was the scene of riots in the North Philadelphia slums—grim testimony to the swiftness of the change from urban growth to urban decay in a much neglected section of the city. Farmland in the distance on the right is the present site of Temple University. This is a sketch by part-time artist David J. Kennedy, a prolific chronicler of Philadelphia scenes in the middle third of the nineteenth century. (Historical Society of Pennsylvania)

AMERICA'S FIRST PHOTOGRAPH was made on October 16, 1839, by Joseph Saxton with a crude camera fashioned from a cigar box. He was an employe of the U. S. Mint, then located on the northwest corner of Chestnut and Juniper streets. The photo was taken from a rear window on the second floor of the mint, with the camera aimed to the northeast across the intersection of Juniper Street and South Penn Square. Many years later, artist Frank H. Taylor portrayed what the camera faintly recorded on a metal plate that historic day. The building in the center of the picture is the original Central High School. The smaller building to the left of the school is the Horse Market Tavern on the southeast corner of Market and Juniper streets. Both buildings were on the present site of the John Wanamaker Department Store. In the left of the picture is a portion of Penn Square, originally Center Square. before the name was changed by the City Council in 1829. (Free Library)

THE NORTHWEST CORNER of Broad and Chestnut streets looked like this in 1841. The Girard Bank is on this site now. (Inquirer)

RIOTS IN 1844 were a tragic and disgraceful episode dramatized in this contemporary print. The Pennsylvania Militia was mobilized in an effort to quell fighting between Catholics and Protestants that raged in the streets of the city and nearby communities sporadically during the spring and summer—leaving more than twenty dead, hundreds wounded, and two Catholic churches destroyed by fire. There was a heavy influx of Irish immigrants to Philadelphia in the early 1840s concurrent with the potato famine in Ireland. An anti-Catholic Native American Party was organized on a platform calling for denial of U. S. citizenship to anyone not born in the United States. This was a prelude to the nation-wide Know-Nothing movement of the 1850s. Party membership soared to more than 4,000 in the Philadelphia area after Catholics protested the reading of the King James version of the Bible in public schools. Initial fighting erupted during a party rally in Kensington, not a part of Philadelphia at that time, and quickly spread. (Free Library)

[33]

HEAD HOUSE at Second and Pine streets, at the head of the old Second Street Market in Society Hill, is shown here on a typically busy day in the 1850s. The mid-street market already was a century old at that time. Head House was built in 1802 as a fire house. Society Hill, rising from the Delaware River in the southeastern part of the city originally laid out by William Penn, derives its name from the Free Society of Traders he chartered to promote the area's settlement and development for prime residential use. It has become an attractive residential section again in recent decades with restoration of old homes and construction of new ones. Head House and the market also have been restored. (Free Library)

[34]

DECLARATION HOUSE, also known as the Graff House, is shown in a deplorable state of neglect in this 1856 photograph. Located on the southwest corner of Seventh and Market streets, it was a newly-built rooming house when Thomas Jefferson wrote the Declaration of Independence in June of 1776, in a second-floor room facing Market Street. Jefferson lived there while a delegate to the Second Continental Congress, which adopted the Declaration on the Fourth of July. The house, which ought to have been preserved as a historic shrine of the first rank, was torn down in 1883. (Free Library)

GIRARD HOUSE, a prominent hotel in the nineteenth century, is the large building on the left in this 1851 photograph looking east on Chestnut Street with the Ninth Street intersection in the foreground. This site later was occupied by part of the Gimbels Department Store. Spires of the old Masonic Temple can be seen farther down Chestnut Street. (Inquirer)

THE FIRST NATIONAL CONVENTION of the Republican Party was held in 1856 at Musical Fund Hall on the south side of Locust Street west of Eighth. The drawing depicts the scene outside the hall as the announcement was made to the waiting crowd that a Presidential nominee had been chosen: John C. Fremont. The election was won by his Democratic opponent, James Buchanan. Musical Fund Hall, opened in 1824, was Philadelphia's foremost concert hall until the Academy of Music was built in 1857. (Inquirer)

ABRAHAM LINCOLN, en route to Washington by train for his first inaugural, stopped in Philadelphia and delivered a Washington's Birthday address in front of Independence Hall on February 22, 1861. He is shown here hoisting a thirty-four-star American Flag, denoting the admission of Kansas to the Union as the thirty-fourth state. (Inquirer)

THE PASSENGER STATION of the Philadelphia and Reading Railroad was at the northeast corner of Broad and Callowhill streets when David Kennedy sketched this scene in 1861. The 401 North Broad Street office building later occupied this site. (Historical Society of Pennsylvania)

THE CONTINENTAL HOTEL was one of the finest in the city when it opened at the southeast corner of Ninth and Chestnut streets shortly before this drawing was made in 1861. (Free Library)

CIVIL WAR RECRUITING for the Union Army reached a feverish pitch in June of 1863 after Confederate forces under General Robert E. Lee launched their invasion of the North. The scene in this contemporary drawing is outside of City Hall at Fifth and Chestnut streets. Philadelphians gave a sigh of relief early in July after Lee had been stopped at a little Pennsylvania town most of them had never heard of before—Gettysburg. (Inquirer)

THE ACADEMY OF MUSIC on the southwest corner of Broad and Locust streets was the site of the 1872 Republican National Convention in which Ulysses S. Grant was nominated for a second term. Modeled after La Scala in Milan, Italy, the Academy has been one of the nation's foremost concert halls since its opening in 1857. With a seating capacity of more than 2,900, it was built for less than $400,000—which may seem almost trivial by present standards, but was an enormous sum at the time. (Inquirer)

"TWO HORSEPOWER" TROLLEY CARS were operating along several routes when this photograph was taken about 1870 on the Second and Third streets line. Horse-drawn trolley service was inaugurated in Philadelphia in 1858, with the first cars operating on Fifth and Sixth streets. But this form of public transportation faded rapidly with the introduction of electric trolley service in 1892. Horses made their last trolley runs in the city in 1897. (Inquirer)

THE CENTENNIAL EXPOSITION grounds are viewed from George's Hill. The three buildings in the foreground are, left to right, Agricultural Hall, Government Hall, and Machinery Hall; the three buildings farther away are, left to right, Horticultural Hall, Memorial Hall, and Main Hall. (Inquirer)

THE CENTENNIAL INTERNATIONAL EXPOSITION in Fairmount Park was opened May 10, 1876, by President Ulysses S. Grant in ceremonies in front of Memorial Hall, the only exposition building that still stands. There were 230,000 people on hand for opening day of the six-month world's fair celebrating the one-hundredth anniversary of the Declaration of Independence. Total attendance was near the ten-million mark by closing day, November 10. The exposition was closed on Sundays. (Inquirer)

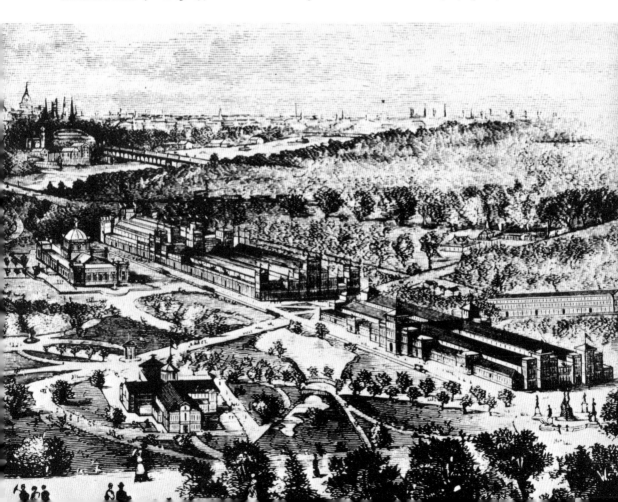

PENN SQUARE had been cleared of trees in preparation for construction of City Hall when this photograph was taken in 1872. The view is from the southwest corner of the square, looking to the northeast. A referendum was held in 1870 to let Philadelphia voters decide whether to build the new City Hall in Penn Square or Washington Square. Penn Square was chosen, 51,000 to 32,000, a decision that had profound effects on the future development of downtown Philadelphia—especially in commercial growth on South Broad Street and preservation of residential neighborhoods in the vicinity of Washington Square. Note that Market and Broad streets intersected in the center of Penn Square, dividing it into four smaller squares. The Pennsylvania Railroad ran trains on tracks in the middle of Market Street. The building under construction on the left across the square is the Masonic Temple on the northeast corner of Broad Street and North Penn Square. To the left of the temple is the Arch Street Methodist Church on the southeast corner of Broad and Arch. (Free Library)

[40]

WEST PHILADELPHIA STATION of the Pennsylvania Railroad was erected in little over two months in 1876 at 32nd and Market Streets to accommodate Centennial Exposition visitors, most of whom arrived and departed by train. The station was destroyed by fire twenty years later. Market Street, running across the full width of the photograph in the foreground, contains tracks used by horse-drawn trolley cars. Posters on the wall at right include advertisements for places of entertainment, one featuring can-can dancers. (Inquirer)

Naughty but Nice: 1883 to 1899

PHILADELPHIA began its third hundred years where the first two left off: growing, growing, growing. The immigrants were pouring in, and they were coming in increasing proportions from eastern and southern Europe. The 1880s were a decade of unprecedented rise in population—nearly 200,000—and the city was over the million mark by the census of 1890. The 1890s were another record breaker, with the population rising almost 250,000. Moreover, there was no end in sight. The twentieth century would bring even more spectacular increases.

The result of rapid growth was rapid change. In the waning years of the nineteenth century, the city blended frontier excitement with Old World charm. For the immigrants, arriving by the hundreds almost every week through most of the 1880s and 1890s, Philadelphia was a frontier of hope and opportunity. Many of the new arrivals were refugees fleeing from poverty or persecution or both. In Philadelphia they were free. They were also poor, but for many of them it was not the extreme poverty they had known before. Their adopted city had become a manufacturing center of great diversity, and jobs were available. The work was hard and the hours were long, but there was money to be made and money to be saved. Thrift was a highly regarded and widely practiced virtue. Family ties tended to be strong. Generations labored and sacrificed and built for future generations. It was a new life, but old traditions were cherished and preserved.

Philadelphia had always been a city of taverns. Now it was a city of saloons. At least that is what they came to be called by the 1890s. Call them what you will—neighborhood taverns or corner saloons—they were everywhere. They proliferated as the city grew, street by street and block by block to the north, to the south, and to the west.

But Philadelphia remained a city of homes. They were erected relentlessly, row by row, and they were bought by families that had never owned homes before and, where they had come from, had never expected to. The front step and, later, the front porch became the symbol of something solid about Philadelphia—a place where families congregated, neighbors laughed and argued, friendships were born, a place where the young and the old and the in-between were comfortable and secure.

Virtually unnoticed amid wave after wave of immigrants from Europe was another kind of population explosion. The number of blacks in Philadelphia doubled between 1880 and 1900, jumping from 31,000 to 62,000. This was due in part to the migration of former slaves and the children of former slaves from the South to the North. It was the result also of a movement from farms and small towns to cities by both blacks and whites—in quest of jobs provided by an industrial revolution that kept shifting into higher and higher gear.

The black migration of the late nineteenth century, however, while producing dramatic growth in Philadelphia's black population, was a drop in the bucket compared with the white migration from Europe. In 1880, the population of Philadelphia was more than 96 percent white. In 1900, it was more than 95 percent white. But the white percentage would never be that high again. A trend had been established, although it wasn't realized at the time, toward a constantly diminishing proportion of whites in the city.

Philadelphia, which had produced America's first schools of medicine and dentistry, pharmacy and law, was by the end of the nineteenth century posting a sizable list of firsts in good things to eat. The soft pretzel, the ice cream cone, the cinnamon bun, scrapple, pepper pot soup—all of these delicacies originated or were popularized in Philadelphia.

The "Gay Nineties" is a term that did not originate in Philadelphia but certainly was applicable to Philadelphia. The city and its people were brimming with optimism as they prepared to welcome a new century.

THE ACADEMY OF MUSIC in the late nineteenth century looked much as it does today, after painstaking restoration work begun in the 1960s. (Free Library)

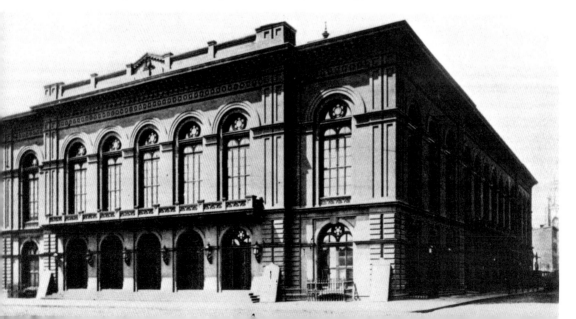

THE PHILLIES introduced major league baseball to Philadelphia with this team in 1883. It was still a strange game to most people and a long way from becoming the national pastime. The Phillies, with a grim hint of things to come, finished last in the National League their first year. (Inquirer)

CITY HALL was the longest continuous news story in Philadelphia during the latter part of the nineteenth century. Although the official ground-breaking ceremony had been held in 1871 and the cornerstone-laying in 1874, the building was not completed until 1901 after some of the citizenry had given up hope that it ever would be. As the cost escalated to a phenomenal $24 million, quite a few taxpayers were hoping it never would be. Most of the 662 rooms were gradually occupied during the 1880s and 1890s, however. This photograph was taken in the 1880s from the southeast corner of Penn Square, looking northwest. The tower had not been completed, but a portion of it is visible to the right of center. The building looks square, but it is not quite. It measures 486 feet from north to south, and 470 feet from east to west. (Free Library)

A WIRE SUSPENSION BRIDGE carried Spring Garden Street across the Schuylkill. The horse-drawn trolley is headed east in this photograph, taken about 1885. On high ground beyond the bridge is a reservoir where the Art Museum stands now. To the left in the background is the old waterworks, built in 1801. (Free Library)

[44]

BROAD STREET STATION of the Pennsylvania Railroad, west of City Hall and north of Market Street, looked like this to incoming passengers in the 1880s. The view is to the east from atop the Chinese Wall at about 17th Street. Tracks approaching the station were elevated, with north-south streets passing underneath through tunnels. The massive structure supporting the tracks originally was dubbed the Chinese Wall with a sense of pride and awe. Later generations thought it was ugly, and "Chinese Wall" then became a derogatory description. The station opened in 1881 but was not fully completed for some years after. The roof is unfinished in this photograph, and there are only a few tracks. Eventually there were sixteen. (Free Library)

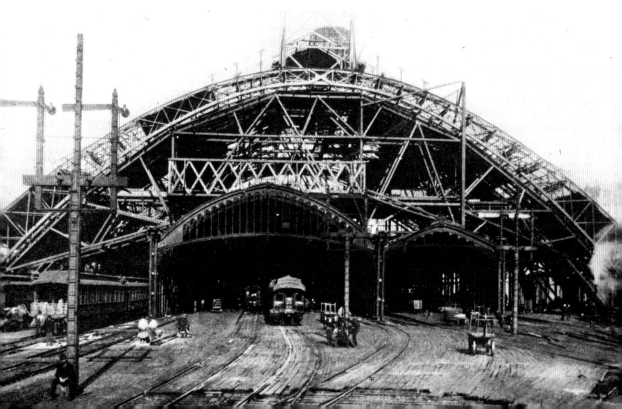

WALNUT STREET had tracks for horse-drawn trolleys in this photo, taken about 1885. The view is to the west from Fourth Street. That's a gas light on the corner at left. The trees in the background are on Independence Square. (Free Library)

REASONABLE PRICES and quality work were featured in business establishments operated by recent-ly arrived immigrants of the late nineteenth century. The shoe repair shop in this 1890 photograph was on Bainbridge Street west of Fifth. That section of South Philadelphia was then known as Little Russia because of the large number of Jewish immigrants from Russia who settled there. (Inquirer)

RIDGWAY HOUSE, on the left, was a Philadelphia landmark for three-quarters of a century. Located on the northwest corner of Market Street and Delaware Avenue, the six-story brick hotel built in the 1850s was used mostly by Delaware River ferry passengers. It was demolished in 1932. An earlier hotel called Ferry House had occupied the site since Colonial times. The view in this photograph, taken in the early 1890s, is looking east on Market Street with the Front Street intersection in the foreground. Cable trolley cars, introduced on Market Street in 1883, are turning around in the loop west of Delaware Ave-nue. The trolleys moved by latching on to a steampowered cable recessed between the rails. The Market Street line was electrified with overhead wires in 1895, but the cable slots between the rails remained for many years. (Inquirer)

THE BLIZZARD of 1888 didn't stop this train from getting through. The famous blizzard of March 11 and 12 dumped ten inches of snow on Philadelphia—the city's biggest snowfall on record at that time—but official weather-record-keeping in Philadelphia did not begin until 1871. The city has had sixteen bigger snowfalls since 1888, but few of them matched the strong winds and high drifts of the 1888 storm. That blizzard was much worse in northern Pennsylvania and in New York City where twice as much snow fell as in Philadelphia. The biggest snowfall on record in Philadelphia is twenty-one inches—in a two-day storm that began on Christmas in 1909. (Free Library)

WEST PHILADELPHIA still had much open country late in the nineteenth century. This double house, shown about 1890, was on the west side of 60th Street in the middle of the 400 block north. There was open space on both sides—with plenty of room for chickens, a garden, and the inevitable outhouse. These two houses later became part of a solid row of houses that filled the entire block. This was not usual procedure, however. In most neighborhoods of West Philadelphia with front-porch row houses, all of the houses in each block were built about the same time. (Miriam Lukens)

[47]

THE BALDWIN LOCOMOTIVE WORKS, already a giant in the early 1890s, but with much expansion yet to come, was located on the west side of Broad Street south of Spring Garden Street. This interior view shows some locomotives in early stages of assembly. (Free Library)

WALNUT STREET offered this view in 1893, looking west with the Third Street intersection in the foreground. Note the increasing signs of advanced civilization—a gas light, mail box, and fire plug huddled together on one corner, and a telephone pole with eleven cross-arms on another. (Inquirer)

COACH AND FOUR was the way to travel in the Gay Nineties. One of the horses remembered to look at the camera. The scene is in front of the Stratford Hotel on the southwest corner of Broad and Walnut streets. The Bellevue Stratford Hotel, built in 1904, is on this site now. In the 1890s, there was a hotel across the street, on the northwest corner of Broad and Walnut, called the Bellevue. (Free Library)

THE WILLIAM PENN STATUE was Philadelphia's most popular attraction in 1893 when it stood in the courtyard of City Hall. Thirty-seven feet tall and weighing nearly twenty-seven tons, the statue was designed by Alexander Calder. Its forty-seven pieces were cast in bronze at the Tacony Iron and Metal Works. The pieces were assembled in the courtyard to make certain they fit properly. In 1894, the statue was partially dismantled and hoisted to the top of City Hall tower in fourteen sections for reassembly. It is still the largest sculpture on any building in the world. City Hall, rising 548 feet to the top of William Penn's hat, is still the highest building in Philadelphia and the world's tallest building without a steel skeleton. The statue faces northeast toward the site in Kensington where Penn made the treaty with the Indians. (Free Library)

CHESTNUT STREET had acquired the look of a busy business thoroughfare by 1893 in this view westward from Eighth Street. (Inquirer)

GLENN WARNER was a football star at Cornell in 1894 when the game resembled trench warfare, and three downs were allowed to advance the ball five yards. Four decades later, then known to everybody as Pop Warner, he was coaching Temple University football teams to national glory. (Inquirer)

BROAD STREET, looking south from City Hall, provided this view in 1896. The Chestnut Street intersection is in the foreground, the Hotel Lafayette on the right. Beyond it, across Sansom Street, the Union League is almost out of sight because of its deep setback from the curb. Beyond the Union League are two more hotels, the Bellevue on the near side of Walnut Street, and the Stratford on the far side of Walnut. (Inquirer)

THE TWO BIGGEST PROJECTS in downtown Philadelphia in the 1880s and 1890s are captured in this one 1895 photograph as both neared completion. Railroad tracks atop the Chinese Wall enter Broad Street Station in the foreground while City Hall rises in the background with the statue of William Penn topping the tower. (Inquirer)

BROAD STREET STATION was the largest railroad station in the world when completed in the 1890s. The arched roof over the sixteen tracks was 600 feet long and nearly 300 feet wide. The station symbolized the power and the glory of the Pennsylvania Railroad when steam was king and trains were the way to travel. This 1897 view is from City Hall, with Market Street extending westward to the left. Among the oldest stories about this terminal is the one about the passenger who asked if the train stopped at Broad Street. "If it doesn't," the conductor replied, "we'll get quite a jolt." (Free Library)

THE FIRST AERIAL PHOTOGRAPH of Philadelphia was made on the Fourth of July in 1893 by William N. Jennings, a local photographer, shortly after taking off in a balloon from the Belmont Plateau section of Fairmount Park in West Philadelphia. With him in the open basket was the pilot, Samuel King. Thousands of spectators saw the free-drifting balloon move eastward as it gained altitude. The view is to the southeast, with the Schuylkill winding through the center of the picture. The zoo is in the foreground on the near side of the river. At the lower left is the Girard Avenue bridge, with part of the nearby railroad bridge also visible. Across the Schuylkill is an observation tower on Lemon Hill. Downstream on the west bank is a lock that carried river traffic past the falls. On the east bank is the waterworks. A new Spring Garden Street bridge is a little farther downstream. To the left of that bridge is the reservoir where the Art Museum stands now. The unfinished tower of City Hall is near the top of the picture in the center. The Delaware River and New Jersey are in the distance. (Inquirer)

"BILLY PENN," as the statue was affectionately known from the beginning, looks serene on his perch atop the City Hall tower in this 1898 photograph. The view is to the west on Market Street with the 11th Street intersection in the foreground. (Free Library)

[53]

THE FAIRMOUNT PARK TROLLEY is ready to start a run in 1896 soon after limited service began. The entire line, meandering over a scenic route of nearly seven miles from 33rd and Dauphin streets to 44th Street and Parkside Avenue, was in operation in 1897. The trolleys crossed the Schuylkill on the Strawberry Mansion Bridge. Woodside Amusement Park, at the edge of Fairmount Park near City Line Avenue, was the most popular trolley stop. Fairmount Park, more than 4,000 acres, grew piece by piece from five acres acquired by the city in 1812. The original acreage, on the east bank of the Schuylkill, includes the present site of the Museum of Art. (Inquirer)

RITTENHOUSE SQUARE was a prime residential area in the nineteenth century, as it still is, but stately mansions stood where apartments houses now rise high. The late-1890s photograph shows the northwest corner of 19th and Walnut Streets. The corner house, facing the square across Walnut Street, was built in the 1840s. The carriage on 19th Street was typical transportation for the wealthy. Passengers rode in an enclosed compartment while the driver braved the elements. (Free Library)

THE WALNUT STREET THEATRE on the northeast corner of Ninth and Walnut streets was already an institution of national renown when this photograph was taken in the 1890s. Virtually every American stage performer of consequence in the nineteenth century appeared here. With a seating capacity of more than 1,000, and recently renovated, it is now the nation's oldest theatre still in use. (Free Library)

Following page: THE BALLOON had moved across the Schuylkill when Jennings took this photo with the camera pointed east. The forty-two-acre campus of Girard College dominates the center of the picture. The campus slashes across streets at odd angles, but most of the streets weren't there when the college opened in 1848 and this part of North Philadelphia was still largely unsettled. In less than half a century the countryside had been transformed into hundreds of blocks of row houses. To the right of Girard College is a reservoir and to the right of that is Eastern State Penitentiary. The Delaware River and New Jersey are at the top of the picture. (Inquirer)

AN AWESOME SIGHT from street level, Broad Street Station looked down from the northwest corner of Market Street and West Penn Square like a medieval castle on the Rhine; note the gingerbread architecture on the tower and along the roof line. At the lower level there was art work galore, competing with the colonnade for the attention of the passersby. The world's largest railroad station was also either the most beautiful or the most outrageous, depending on one's point of view, and it was directly across the street from City Hall, a mammoth pile of stone and sculpture so formidable that Broad Street Station looked almost plain by comparison. There were some who said the two buildings deserved each other. In any case, the railroad station, as City Hall, symbolized solid confidence in a secure future as the twentieth century beckoned. If anyone had stood in front of Broad Street Station when this photograph was taken in 1899 and predicted that the Pennsylvania Railroad someday would enter into a disastrous merger and subsequently declare bankruptcy, he would have been carted away as one who surely had taken leave of his senses. (Inquirer)

Innocence and Idealism: 1900 to 1918

LINCOLN STEFFENS, the renowned commentator on urban ills in the early twentieth century, described Philadelphia in 1903 as "corrupt and contented." It was a fair appraisal if put in proper perspective. Far more Philadelphians were contented than corrupt.

The corruption was primarily in politics and business, often hand in hand. The first two decades of the century brought phenomenal changes in ways of life. Electric lighting, which had been introduced in the 1880s, began replacing gas as the principal source of illumination after the turn of the century. The telephone, which also had made its debut in the late 1800s, emerged as a widely used means of communication in the early 1900s. Electric trolleys, which had made their initial appearance in the 1890s, were a rapidly expanding form of public transportation. Asphalt paving of streets, begun in the 1890s, spread swiftly in the decades that followed. Revolutionary advances in indoor plumbing were accompanied by massive construction of sewer and water lines and waste disposal facilities. Simultaneously with all this, there was unprecedented population growth, with vast new sections of the city undergoing rapid residential, business, and industrial development. Old fortunes were multiplied, and new fortunes were made in the supplying of all of these urban needs through mammoth public works, public utility projects, and private building. Contracts and franchises worth millions upon millions were awarded. The temptation for fraud and favoritism was hard for some to resist. It was not always resisted.

The contentment was mostly among people of modest circumstances who were far removed from the political and business arena of wheeling and dealing. No doubt those growing rich were contented, too, but there was a different kind of wealth in the row houses. The Americanization of the immigrants who had poured into Philadelphia in the nineteenth century was in full tilt as the twentieth began. The process of assimilation strengthened with each succeeding generation. New immigrants who arrived in still rising numbers had the advantage of comfort and counsel from earlier arrivals who had jobs, homes, and families, and had learned from experience that the American dream wasn't just a dream but was real.

Moral fiber toughened. The Roman Catholic Church, which had played an increasing role in spiritual leadership in the eighteenth and nineteenth centuries, met the challenges of the twentieth with vigorous expansion. Roman Catholic High School, which had opened in 1890 as the first free Catholic high school in the country, proved to be the forerunner of enormous growth in Catholic education in the city. Synagogues grew in number and membership as immigration by Jews increased, many of them refugees from persecution in Europe. Protestant denominations, many of them firmly rooted since soon after the city's founding, attained new levels of enrollment and community activity.

Philadelphia's population exceeded one and one-half million in the census of 1910 after a record-shattering gain of more than a quarter of a million during the first decade of the twentieth century. But even that record would be broken in the second decade as the tide of immigration seemed to know no end. South Philadelphia was growing rapidly with arrivals from Italy. Completion of the Market Street Subway-Elevated nourished a home-building boom in West Philadelphia within walking distance north and south of Market. The new residential areas spawned neighborhood shopping districts on 52nd and 60th streets, and on Market Street itself. Residential growth to the north pushed to Olney Avenue and beyond. Along the river from center-city toward the northeast, remaining open space as far as Tacony was turning into blocks of row homes.

World War I spurred Philadelphia's growth. The flow of immigrants from Europe increased. During the nineteen months of U. S. participation in the conflict in 1917 and 1918, employment opportunities in war-related industries attracted job hunters to the city. Shipbuilding experienced an especially spectacular boom.

Some other cities were growing even faster—Chicago, for example, which by 1900 had replaced Philadelphia as the nation's second-largest city. But Philadelphia kept advancing onward and upward—in both material goods and in human spirit—as a city of homes and families, of factories and jobs. Whatever corruption existed, in places high or low, had not corrupted the faith of the populace. Philadelphia not only was contented. It was confident.

MARKET STREET in 1900, looking east from City Hall, provided a blend of trolley cars and horse-drawn vehicles. The building on the right, part of which is taller than the rest and has the clock tower on top, was the old John Wanamaker Department Store. (Free Library)

ONE DIME would buy a lot of entertainment around the turn of the century at Ninth and Arch. (Free Library)

THE JOHN WANAMAKER Department Store, shown here in 1901, has occupied the same site on the south side of Market Street east of City Hall since 1876. The Pennsylvania Railroad had built a freight station at this location in 1853, but approaching tracks on Market Street through Penn Square were ripped up when City Hall was built. John Wanamaker, the store's founder, was postmaster general from 1889 to 1893 in the Cabinet of President Benjamin Harrison. (Free Library)

[62]

LONG DRESSES didn't prevent women from riding bicycles in 1900. This is Broad Street, looking north. The nearest building on the left is the old Hotel Bellevue on the northwest corner of Broad and Walnut. Taller buildings in the distance were considered skyscrapers at the dawn of the twentieth century. (Inquirer)

THIS MANSION, built in 1839, still occupied the northeast corner of Broad and Walnut streets in 1901. It was the home of members of the Lippincott book-publishing family for many years. The trolley is on Walnut Street. In the background is the Witherspoon Building. (Free Library)

THE CONTINENTAL HOTEL on the southeast corner of Ninth and Chestnut streets was still a fairly classy establishment in 1902, but was on the decline. It was demolished in 1926 and replaced by the Benjamin Franklin Hotel. The vendor in that horse-drawn wagon parked on Ninth Street is selling spring water for a penny a glass—a popular item at a time when Philadelphia water was considered distasteful by many, especially out-of-towners not used to it. Repairs at intersections already were becoming a typical scene in the city—a perennial price paid for the comfort and convenience of paved streets and sewer and water lines. (Inquirer)

THE OLDEST FINE ARTS institution in the United States, the Pennsylvania Academy of Fine Arts was established in 1805 with distinguished artist Charles Willson Peale among the founders. George Clymer, a signer of the Declaration of Independence, was the first president. This 1901 photograph shows an art class in the Academy's school and museum at the southwest corner of Broad and Cherry streets. The building still looks much as it did when completed in 1876. (Inquirer)

THEODORE ROOSEVELT, who at the age of forty-two had become the nation's youngest president when William McKinley was assassinated the year before, was the principal speaker at the dedication of a new Central High School at Broad and Green streets in 1902. (Inquirer)

BROAD STREET was sufficiently free of traffic in 1904 to permit these two boys to pose for the photographer. The view is to the north. The first building on the left is the brand-new Bellevue Stratford Hotel on the southwest corner of Broad and Walnut. Parked at the curb on the left is a revolutionary mode of transportation—an automobile. Beyond the Bellevue Stratford, across Walnut Street, the old Bellevue Hotel still stands. Also on the left is the twenty-two-story Land Title Building, completed in 1902. On the right the first tall structure is the North American Building. A major Philadelphia newspaper for many years, the *North American* ceased publication in 1925. (Inquirer)

TROLLEYS were the way to travel in the early 1900s, and riders sometimes had a choice of closed or open. The open-air trolley on the Eighth Street line *(above)* was a nice way to enjoy a shopping trip to center-city department stores such as Lit Brothers, shown here, at Eighth and Market. The advertising poster on the trolley serves notice that visitors to Willow Grove Amusement Park in Montgomery County may enjoy the music of Walter Damrosch. Although the open trolley sometimes got a bit crowded, as on the Richmond Street line *(below)*, there always seemed to be room for one more if he didn't mind hanging on. (Inquirer)

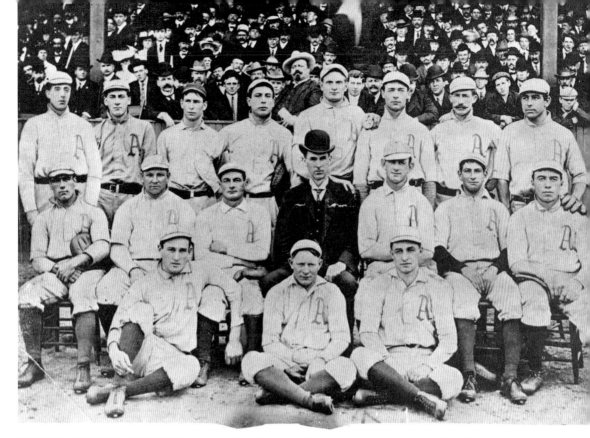

THE PHILADELPHIA ATHLETICS were the city's first major league pennant winners when they finished first in the American League in 1902. Manager Connie Mack is in the second row, center. The most famous players on the team were two pitchers, Eddie Plank (third row, left) and Rube Waddell (third row, directly behind Mack). The photo was taken at Columbia Park, 29th Street and Columbia Avenue, where the A's played before Shibe Park was built in 1909. (Inquirer)

THE PHILLIES WON their first National League pennant in 1915 after thirty-three years of trying. It would be thirty-five years more before they would win another. The star of the team was pitcher Grover Cleveland Alexander (center row, fourth from the left) who retired in 1930 with a career total of 373 victories, never since equalled in the major leagues. Two pitchers who had retired earlier, Cy Young and Walter Johnson, won more games, and another, Christy Mathewson, won the same number. Pat Moran, to the right of Alexander, was the manager of the 1915 Phillies. Another pitcher on that team, Stan Baumgartner (back row, second from the left), later was for many years a sportswriter for the *Philadelphia Inquirer*. The Phillies lost to the Boston Red Sox in the World Series, four games to one. (Inquirer)

CONNIE MACK was the best-dressed as well as the most durable manager in the history of baseball—and he was never without that trusty scorecard he used to signal his players from the dugout. He is shown here shaking hands with manager John McGraw of the New York Giants before the first game of the 1911 World Series. The Philadelphia Athletics won the series in six games to become the first American League team to win the world championship two consecutive years. After a sixteen-year playing career as a catcher with other teams. Mack came to Philadelphia in 1901 to begin a half-century as manager of the A's. He led them to nine American League and five world championships—all in a thirty-year span from 1902 to 1931. Shibe Park at 20th Street and Lehigh Avenue, where the A's and later the Phillies played, was renamed Connie Mack Stadium in 1953. (Inquirer)

FOOTBALL WAS REVOLUTIONIZED in 1906 when President Theodore Roosevelt, appalled by a mounting toll of deaths and crippling injuries, demanded that the game be made more humane. The rules were changed to abolish the massing of players in giant wedges for charges against their foe; the forward pass was introduced; and teams were required to advance the ball ten yards in three downs, in stead of five yards in three downs, to retain possession. The photograph of the 1906 University of Pennsylvania football team illustrates the results. With the game opened up, speed and agility were the requisites, rather than brute strength. These footballers with the lean look were the beginning of an era in which Penn was a pioneer in developing the game as a glamorous spectator sport. The Saturday afternoon hero was about to be born and Penn was ready, having built Franklin Field as the nation's first horseshoe stadium in 1904. It was the predecessor of the present stadium with the same name, built in the 1920s. Penn played in the second Rose Bowl game in 1917, when it was known as the Pasadena Bowl, losing to Oregon, 14-0. (Inquirer)

THE UNION LEAGUE, venerable bastion of Republicanism, left no doubt where it stood during the celebration of the fiftieth anniversary of the Republican Party in 1906. The club house at Broad and Sansom was decorated with banners bearing the names of Republican Presidential nominees. (Free Library)

BROAD STREET, looking north about 1905 with the Girard Avenue intersection in the foreground, was a prime residential area. The mansion on the corner at the left was the home of members of the Widener family, and later became the Widener Branch of the Free Library. (Historical Society of Pennsylvania)

THE METROPOLITAN OPERA HOUSE on the southwest corner of Broad and Poplar streets was a magnificent structure inside and out when it opened in 1908. Its 4,000 seating capacity featured exquisitely furnished boxes for the city's wealthiest families, many of whom lived on North Broad Street. Oscar Hammerstein, the great opera producer and grandfather of his namesake who was to become a part of the Rodgers and Hammerstein Broadway musical team, was the guiding genius behind the Met, as it was popularly known. He presented eighty operas a season in the opening years. The Metropolitan Opera Company of New York gave its Philadelphia performances in the Met for fifteen years. But by the late 1920s, the neighborhood was starting to decline and so was the Met. The Academy of Music, a half-century older and a couple of miles south on Broad Street, regained primacy in the Philadelphia opera scene. (Free Library)

THE GIRARD BANK was called the Girard Trust Company when it erected this beautiful headquarters that still stands on the northwest corner of Broad and Chestnut streets. Shown here soon after it was completed in 1908, the building was modeled after the Pantheon in Rome. Note how clean and uncluttered the corner is, only slightly marred by an unobtrusive fire plug. Soon this would change, all over the city, as automotive traffic brought signal lights, directional signs, no-parking signs, and bus-stop markers to heavily traveled intersections. (Inquirer)

SUBWAY CONSTRUCTION required sections of Market Street to be closed for varying periods in the early 1900s. This section, east of Second Street, had just been reopened to traffic in 1908 but was not yet resurfaced. The Market Street Subway, from Delaware Avenue to 22nd Street, was the city's first. Subway trains continued westward on an elevated structure to 69th Street in Delaware County. Construction began in 1903, and trains began running in 1907 on the portion of the line west of City Hall. In the following year, the remainder of the subway went into service, along with an elevated extension that carried trains on Delaware Avenue between Market and South streets. The entire project was built and financed by the Philadelphia Rapid Transit Company, which made substantial profits even though the fare was held to eight cents (fifteen cents for a round trip) until 1947. The city built the elevated extension to Bridge Street in Frankford and leased it to PRT, with service beginning in 1922. The elevated line on Market Street between 22nd and 44th streets was replaced by a subway in the 1950s. Some of the original 1907 subway cars were in operation until 1961. (Inquirer)

JOHN WANAMAKER'S new building, the one still in use at the southeast corner of Market Street and East Penn Square, was the world's largest department store when it opened in 1911. The top photo, taken in 1916, shows Wanamaker Field on the roof—featuring tracks for sprinting and long-distance running, along with basketball and tennis courts. In the photo on the facing page, taken about the same time, the motorized delivery fleet is lined up at the store. (Inquirer)

A PEDESTRIAN BRIDGE had been built across Market Street for Broad Street Station passengers and employes by 1910 to help them cope with what at the time was considered heavy traffic—a mixture of horse-drawn vehicles, trolley cars, and automobiles. The photograph was taken from a window of City Hall, with portions of City Hall visible at the right. (Free Library)

CITY OFFICIALS lost no time in recognizing the comfort and convenience of modern automotive transportation. These cars were lined up on the west side of City Hall in 1910. Broad Street Station is across the street. Note the electric street lights in front of City Hall on the right and also across the street on the left. (Inquirer)

READING TERMINAL at 12th and Market streets, shown here about 1910, was a handsome rival to the Pennsylvania Railroad's Broad Street Station less than three blocks away. Completed in 1893, the Reading Railroad's center-city showpiece covered its track area with an arched roof 507 feet long and 267 feet wide—not quite as large as the Pennsy's roof but respectably close. And the Reading had its Terminal Market, a fairyland of good things to eat, as an added attraction. The *Inquirer's* old building on Market Street can be seen at the right. (Free Library)

THE BALTIMORE AND OHIO Railroad Station on the south side of Chestnut Street west of 24th, in about 1910, is shown in this view facing east. The railing on the right is at the eastern end of the Chestnut Street Bridge across the Schuylkill. Railroad rivalry that had been keen in the latter part of the nineteenth century in Philadelphia became even more so in the early decades of the twentieth. This station opened in 1888 but was destroyed by fire in 1926, four years after B&O passenger service to Philadelphia had been abandoned. (Inquirer)

A REPAIR TOWER drawn by horses was used by the Philadelphia Rapid Transit Company to service overhead lines. That's an open-air trolley in the background. (Inquirer)

MAGNOLIA BLOSSOMS were never more beautiful than they were in the spring of 1911 to these fascinated kindergarten youngsters. The scene is on the twenty-one-acre West Philadelphia campus of the Overbrook School for the Blind. (Free Library)

JERSEY SEASHORE resorts were attracting many Philadelphians early in the twentieth century, but beaches and boardwalks were still uncrowded and there were no traffic jams. Bathing suits greatly limited suntan opportunities, as this 1913 photograph at Ocean City shows. Boardwalk onlookers were amply attired also. (Wilson)

GYMNASTS were almost as well-dressed as the proud parents looking on at the Field Day conducted by the public schools in the Belmont Plateau section of Fairmount Park in 1914. (Free Library)

GARBAGE TRUCKS with sliding steel covers were featured in the modernization program of the Department of Public Works in 1918. The DPW also encouraged personal cleanliness with its Public Baths and Wash House on Gaskill Street in South Philadelphia. Many households did not yet enjoy the luxury of their own bath and wash tubs. (Free Library)

FRANKLIN D. ROOSEVELT, looking dapper in a derby, was a handsome, young assistant secretary of the Navy when he inspected Naval installations in Philadelphia during World War I. (Inquirer)

BOIES PENROSE, who stood 6' 4" and weighed nearly 300, was also a giant in city, state, and national politics. After serving for twelve years as a state legislator from Philadelphia, he was a U. S. senator from 1897 until his death in 1921. A member of an old and wealthy Philadelphia family, he preferred the smoke-filled room to the drawing room and became the most powerful, although not unchallenged, Republican Party boss in Pennsylvania. His idea of a hearty breakfast was a dozen eggs to go with a large slice of ham, a dozen rolls, and five or six cups of coffee. (Inquirer)

[80]

TRUCKS began to appear on Philadelphia streets not long after the arrival of the first automobiles. Lit Brothers had inaugurated motorized deliveries by the time this photograph was taken, about 1912. (Free Library)

Boom and Bust: 1919 to 1941

BETWEEN THE two World Wars Philadelphia, along with the rest of the nation, had good times and bad times of almost equal length, with the stock market crash of 1929 as the dividing line. Everything was coming up roses in the Twenties. Hopes and dreams were falling apart in the Thirties.

But there was more continuity to the era in Philadelphia than in many cities. The period of maximum growth for Philadelphia had already passed when the Twenties began. Rising expectations were not as sharply inclined as elsewhere, and the downward plunge in the Thirties consequently was not so precipitous. The city already had matured and it managed to roll with the punch in 1929.

This is not to deny that there was euphoria before and hardship after the crash. The painful adjustment from prosperity to Depression was blunted, however, by the exceptionally wide diversification of the city's economy. Philadelphia was at one and the same time a great seaport and a great railroad center, a manufacturing city making a variety of products from hats and candy to cigars and machinery, a city of far-ranging service industries including insurance, banking, and printing, a city with a mixture of government installations and private enterprise. There were happy times and there were sad times, but the city which had already seen much of both in its first two-and-a-half centuries took it all in stride.

The most fundamental change to take place during this period was that, for the first time since William Penn had arrived in 1682, the city stopped growing. The decade ending in 1920 brought the most rapid population growth in the city's history—nearly 275,000. But immigration from Europe dropped off dramatically in the 1920s, followed by a decline in the birthrate during the Depression of the 1930s. The population of 1,823,000 in 1920 rose only modestly to 1,950,000 in 1930, a gain of 127,000. In the next ten years it dropped 19,000 to 1,931,000. That was the first decline ever recorded in the city—but it was not to be the last. Although there were interim ups as well as downs, Philadelphia in 1970 would have 863 fewer inhabitants than it had forty years earlier, in 1930.

This is only half the story, however, and does not in itself convey the whole picture. The Philadelphia Metropolitan Area—which is to say the city and the suburbs combined—grew rapidly through this period. Suburban growth, which had been substantial even before World War I, accelerated between the wars and became explosive after World War II. The basic characteristic of the city as a more or less self-contained economic unit thus was undergoing revolutionary change during the Twenties and Thirties. More and more people who worked in Philadelphia did not live there. Early suburban growth was predominantly in Delaware and Montgomery counties. South Jersey suburban development began with the completion of the Delaware River Bridge in 1926. Bucks and Chester counties for the most part did not feel the impact of the suburbs until later.

While the automobile was instrumental in transforming Philadelphia into a city surrounded by suburbs, it was by no means the only factor. The decision to terminate the Market Street Subway-Elevated at 69th Street in Upper Darby Township instead of 63rd Street in Philadelphia, contributed directly to development of Upper Darby as the most populous suburb in the metropolitan area. It also led to development of the 69th Street retail shopping area in the 1920s, which quickly overshadowed West Philadelphia business districts on 52nd and 60th streets, and also siphoned off business from center-city. By the 1930s, thousands of city residents in West Philadelphia were going to the suburbs, specifically to 69th Street, to shop, reversing the traditional pattern of suburbanites coming to the city to shop.

Railroads contributed mightily to suburban growth, most notably along the main line of the Pennsylvania Railroad to the west—from which the suburban area known as the Main Line derives its name. Early suburban growth in Delaware County, aside from Upper Darby, was concentrated around railroad stations on the Pennsy's main line to the south, and on its commuter line to Media.

Nearly all of the city residents moving to the suburbs in the 1920s and 1930s were white. Meanwhile, black migration into the city, mostly but not entirely from the South, continued. The black population of Philadelphia, seven percent in 1920, rose to 11 percent in 1930, and 13 percent in 1940. The city's black inhabitants had passed the quarter-million mark by 1940.

As Philadelphians entered the 1940s, they began to emerge from the Great

Depression. But before they could give a sigh of relief, war clouds were gathering on the horizon.

BILLY became an instant hit with the small fry when the bronze statue was installed in Rittenhouse Square in 1919. Philadelphia, already renowned for its statues and fountains, enhanced that reputation throughout the first half of the twentieth century by developing enormous variety in subject matter for statuary in parks and squares. (Free Library)

THIS DOUBLE-DECKER, called a Boulevard Bus, was the latest thing in public transportation when it went on display at City Hall in 1922. Double-deckers went into regular service in Philadelphia in 1923 and were mainstays of the city's surface transportation system for more than a quarter-century, even though the conventional single-deck buses were introduced in 1924. (Inquirer)

[83]

FRIVOLITIES of 1920 at the Chestnut Street Opera House, on the north side between 10th and 11th, received complimentary reviews from seven Philadelphia newspapers. Carefully chosen excerpts had been put on display, at the left, by the theatre's management. The best seats in the house were $1.50 for matinees, and on week nights you could get in for as little as 50 cents. (Inquirer)

MUMMERS have been a Philadelphia tradition since Colonial times, and their origin in Europe goes back to antiquity. Early Philadelphia mummers, brightly costumed and often masked, engaged in holiday revelry during the Christmas-New Year season on an informal basis in their own neighborhoods. Groups of mummers began parading to center-city and to other neighborhoods in the 1870s. The present custom of combining into one big parade on New Year's Day began in 1901. Shown here is the Trilby String Band ready to march up Broad Street in the 1920 parade. Costuming would become much more elaborate in years ahead. (Inquirer)

THE RITZ CARLTON, built in 1911 on the southeast corner of Broad and Walnut streets, was one of the city's leading hotels when this photograph was taken in the early 1920s. The site is now occupied by the Pennsylvania Lumbermen's Mutual Building, with a Horn & Hardart restaurant on the first floor. (Free Library)

BROAD STREET STATION was swept by a spectacular fire in its train-shed area on June 11, 1923. The top photo shows firemen fighting the blaze from the Market Street side. The view in the bottom photo is from Filbert Street, now John F. Kennedy Boulevard. Under construction, in the background at right, is the Fox Theater building on the southwest corner of 16th and Market streets. (Free Library)

SERVICE WAS RESTORED at Broad Street Station Wednesday morning, June 13, 1923 *(above)*, only about thirty-six hours after the fire had been extinguished. Passengers walked from the western end of the shed area to the waiting room gates on a temporary platform. The station was a terminal for commuter as well as inter-city trains before Suburban Station was opened in 1930. Several weeks after the fire *(below)* all sixteen tracks were back in service. The entire floor in the 600-foot-long shed area had been replaced, along with all platforms, track beds, tracks, lighting, and signal systems. The steel framework that had supported the wooden shed roof was later torn down, and an individual low-level roof was built over each passenger platform. This view is to the west, in the direction of departing trains. (Free Library)

[87]

BROAD STREET SUBWAY construction was under way in 1925, creating serious traffic problems but providing delight for sidewalk superintendents. The view is north, toward the intersection with Vine Street, which had not yet been widened to a ten-lane highway. Nearest building on the left is the Hahnemann Medical College and Hospital. It is on a portion of the site now occupied by that institution's

twenty-story main hospital building, completed in 1929. Farther up the street on the left, where the sign says "Lunch," is a Horn & Hardart Automat. The Elks Lodge in the next block is the same building now occupied by the Philadelphia Athletic Club. Beyond the Elks Lodge a part of the brand-new Inquirer building can be seen. (Inquirer)

GUSTINE LAKE in Fairmount Park, a popular place to swim for generations of Philadelphians, often attracted a goodly number of non-swimmers, too. Just getting your feet wet was fun in the 1920s, as always. (Free Library)

MUNICIPAL STADIUM at Broad Street and Pattison Avenue was under construction in 1925. The name was changed to Philadelphia Stadium in 1959 and to John F. Kennedy Stadium in 1964. Originally designed to seat 86,000 for Sesqui-Centennial Exposition events in 1926, the stadium now has a capacity of 102,000 for Army-Navy football games with the use of movable field seats on the inner rim of the horseshoe. Note the double-decker buses on Broad Street. (Free Library)

SUNDAY DRIVES in the park were becoming a popular form of recreation in 1924, but passengers in open touring cars had to bundle up in cold weather. The little fellow on the left is the author of this book. The auto is a 1923 Studebaker. (Wilson)

THE CHINESE WALL *(right)* was appropriately named, as this 1925 photograph shows. Building an elevated structure to support sixteen railroad tracks and the trains that ran on them was an impressive engineering accomplishment in the 1880s. The view is to the north directly through the 16th Street tunnel. Note the policeman under an umbrella at the left directing traffic at 16th and Market with a manually-operated stop-and-go signal. The top stories of the Insurance Company of North America building at 16th and Arch streets can be seen in the distance. (Free Library)

FILBERT STREET, looking west from a point near 15th Street, is shown in this 1925 photograph *(below)*. That's the Chinese Wall on the left, somewhat altered after the 1923 Broad Street Station fire. A photograph taken at the same spot today would show a much wider John F. Kennedy Boulevard with Kennedy Plaza on the right and Penn Center office buildings on the left. (Free Library)

THE SESQUI-CENTENNIAL EXPOSITION, com-
memorating the one-hundred-fiftieth anniversary of
American independence, was opened on May 31, 1926,
by Secretary of State Frank B. Kellogg (left), shown
leaving City Hall for the exposition grounds with
Mayor William F. Kendrick. Ceremonies were held in
Municipal Stadium. The bottom photo, looking north
from inside the exposition grounds, shows the giant
reproduction of the Liberty Bell that straddled Broad
Street at the entrance. In its six-month run, closing
December 1, the exposition drew more than six million
people. (Inquirer)

HAVING FUN was as much a part of going to the Sesqui as looking at educational and historical exhibits in such buildings as the Palace of Liberal Arts, the Palace of Agriculture, the Palace of Education, the Palace of Fine Arts, and the Pennsylvania State building. The Cyclone Coaster *(above)* guaranteed speeds of more than 100 miles per hour. It was a fearsome ride that was supposed to separate the men from the boys, but that brave woman in the front car seems to be taking it all rather calmly. Below is a general view of the amusement area, which offered five rides for 50 cents. (Inquirer)

TAKING NO CHANCES, the Philadelphia Fire Department had equipment and personnel on the exposition grounds around the clock. (Inquirer)

THE DELAWARE RIVER BRIDGE *(facing page)*, later renamed the Benjamin Franklin Bridge, was the longest suspension bridge (1.8 miles) in the United States when it opened July 1, 1926. With no vehicles allowed on opening day, this was the scene as thousands from both sides of the river enjoyed the once-in-a-lifetime opportunity to stroll leisurely along the traffic lanes. The photo below shows toll booths at the New Jersey end of the bridge after it was opened to traffic. The toll was 25 cents. (Inquirer)

FERRIES hung on for twenty-six years after the bridge opened, although fewer of them operated and they suffered an immediate loss of customers. However, as this photo shows, taken just a few days after the bridge opened, there were still plenty of people riding the ferries. (Inquirer)

BRIDGE POLICE acquired a patrol car and a motorcycle less than three weeks after the span opened. They were bad news for speeders. (Inquirer)

AN *Inquirer* AIRPLANE became the first to fly under the bridge, three weeks after it opened. The center span is 135 feet above the water. (Inquirer)

A NAVY DIRIGIBLE, the *Los Angeles,* flew over the Delaware River Bridge in August of 1926 on a training flight from its base in Lakehurst, New Jersey. The 650-foot-long airship with sleeping accommodations for thirty people was built for the United States at the Zeppelin works in Germany in 1924. It made 250 successful flights, many of them over the Philadelphia area or the Jersey seashore, before retiring of old age in 1932. It was one of the few dirigibles that managed to avoid disaster. (Inquirer)

LET'S GO, PENN! With completion of a new Franklin Field in 1925, the University of Pennsylvania had the first double-deck stadium on any campus in America. With the addition of end-zone seats at the open end of the horseshoe, the Quakers played to home crowds of up to 80,000 in their heyday, for many years leading the nation in home-game season attendance. The development of intersectional rivalries was stressed, most notably with Notre Dame and Michigan, and emphasis was placed on making football a spectacle—with the aid of cheerleaders, marching bands, and half-time extravaganzas. The Penn cheerleaders in this photograph were whooping it up in the 1925 game against Swarthmore. The tiny suburban college in Delaware County fielded phenomenal football teams for its size, and for a number of years provided early season tests for Penn. (Inquirer)

PENN PIONEERED in the development of large football coaching staffs with assistants assigned to highly specialized duties. The 1926 staff consisted of seven coaches plus a physician and a trainer. Lou Young, third from left, was head coach. To the right of Young is Bert Bell, backfield coach, who acquired a National Football League franchise for Philadelphia in 1933 and founded the Eagles. The old Frankford Yellow Jackets had represented the city in the NFL from 1924 to 1931. From 1944 until his death in 1959, Bell was commissioner of the National Football League. He collapsed and died while watching a game in Philadelphia between the Eagles and the Pittsburgh Steelers. (Inquirer)

BROAD STREET RESURFACING had begun late in 1926 in this section, looking south from Callow-hill Street, after subway construction. Temporary wooden planking carried traffic before the resurfacing. A gas main, foreground, was elevated over Broad Street while the subway was being dug. Several taxis can be seen in the traffic down the street. The building beyond the one with a "rent" sign is Roman Catholic High School, the first free Catholic High School in the country, which still stands on the northeast corner of Broad and Vine. The Broad Street Subway between Olney Avenue and City Hall was completed in 1928. (Inquirer)

A HISTORY-MAKING CROWD of 120,757 jammed into Municipal Stadium on the night of September 23, 1926, during the Sesqui-Centennial celebration, to see the first Dempsey-Tunney fight. It still stands as a world record for paid attendance at a boxing match. This photograph was taken before the fighters had entered the ring. Gene Tunney won a ten-round decision to end Jack Dempsey's seven-year reign as heavyweight champion. (Inquirer)

THE ART MUSEUM, to become one of the nation's greatest cultural institutions as well as one of its most beautiful buildings, is under construction at the top right of this 1926 aerial photograph showing the Benjamin Franklin Parkway extending from City Hall through Logan Square to the museum. The traffic circle has been built on Logan Square. On the north side of the square the Free Library of Philadelphia is nearing completion. Broad Street Station and the Chinese Wall are behind City Hall tower. (Free Library)

THE RECLINING INDIAN, a part of the Washington Monument statuary in front of the Art Museum, seems to be contemplating the many changes that have taken place in Philadelphia, as he gazes down the Benjamin Franklin Parkway toward City Hall in 1927. (Inquirer)

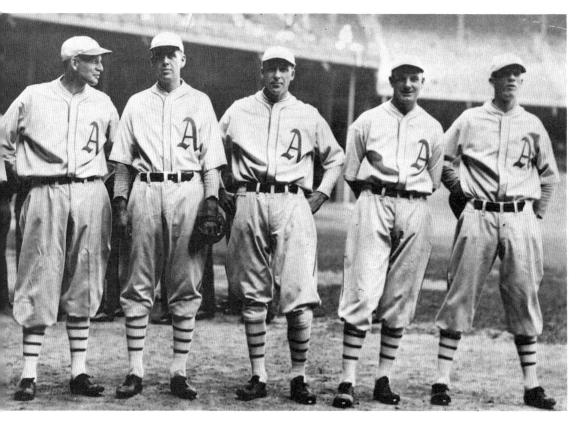

THE GREATEST TEAM ever to have
played the game of baseball is what some
oldtimers still call the Philadelphia Athletics that won three straight American
League pennants in 1929 through 1931,
at a time when other teams also had line-
ups heavily saturated with superstars.
These 1929 photographs show some of
the outstanding A's of that era. The pitch-
ing staff *(above)* included, left to right,
Howard Ehmke, George Earnshaw, Rube
Walberg, Eddie Rommel, and Lefty Grove.
The team also had awesome power at the
plate, including *(left)* Mickey Cochrane,
Al Simmons, Mule Haas, and Jimmy Foxx,
from left to right, who were known as
Mack's Mighty Four. This was manager
Connie Mack's last great team that dom-
inated baseball in a period when they had
to be good to beat the powerful New
York Yankees led by Babe Ruth. (Inqui-
rer)

THE MASTBAUM THEATER *(above)* on the northwest corner of 20th and Market streets is shown on February 24, 1929, three days before it opened. It was the third largest theater in the world, with a seating capacity of more than 5,000, and heralded the golden age of motion pictures. It provided for movie goers an opulence and grandeur that no vaudeville or play house could match. The foyer and lounges featured crystal, gold leaf, and mirrors in lavish decorations. The orchestra pit *(below)*, in the foreground, accommodated fifty pieces. The Mastbaum, completed only eight months before the stock-market crash that began the Great Depression, was classic Roaring-Twenties architecture in the field of entertainment. But for all its richness, it was not gaudy. It was the place to go in Philadelphia in the pre-television era when talking pictures were the No. 1 form of mass entertainment, and going to the movies was more American than apple pie. When it was built, it looked sturdy enough to stand a thousand years, but it lasted only twenty-nine. The wrecker's ball reduced it to dust in 1958—a casualty of television, changing fashions, and less formal lifestyles. (Inquirer)

Preceding page: THE SCHUYLKILL winds its way through this 1927 aerial photograph from below the Spring Garden Street Bridge, in the foreground, northward to suburban Montgomery County, in the distance. The Art Museum, already under construction eight years, was only a year away from its grand opening. Boat House Row can be seen upstream from the museum. Across the river, below the Girard Avenue Bridge, is the zoo. Eastern State Penitentiary, its cell blocks resembling the spokes of a wheel, is at the lower right. The main building of Girard College is just above it. Fairmount Park dominates the center of the photo. (Inquirer)

THE FIRST RADIO BROADCAST of a Philadelphia Orchestra concert from the Academy of Music was on October 6, 1929, and it was relayed by mobile transmitter so that the people assembled on Reyburn Plaza, where the Municipal Services Building now stands, could enjoy a concert in the park. That's Broad Street Station in the background. (Inquirer)

BIG BILL TILDEN was Philadelphia's greatest tennis player of all time, and he was the world's best during the golden age of sports in the 1920s. He is shown here (on the left) serving to Vin Richards in 1931 during a professional indoor match at the Philadelphia Arena at 46th and Market streets. He won the U. S. pro singles championship that year at the age of thirty-eight. In younger years, as an amateur, he won the national singles title seven times—including six in a row. Long trousers were the standard dress for tennis players in those days. (Inquirer)

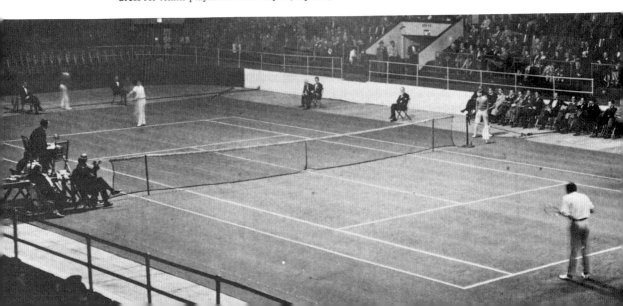

WILLIAM S. VARE, with cane, was greeted by a huge throng of loyal supporters when he arrived at Broad Street Station in 1929 after the U. S. Senate had refused to seat him, thus ending a three-year battle that was one of the most remarkable episodes in the nation's political history. Bill Vare was the leader of the Vare Boys, a family of political bosses that had feuded with Boies Penrose for control of the Republican Party in Philadelphia for many years, and had finally emerged victorious with Penrose's death in 1921. One of ten children of an immigrant pig farmer, Bill Vare started out as a messenger boy for John Wanamaker's department store at $1.50 a week. He had reached the pinnacle of political power in 1926 when, in the Republican primary, he challenged incumbent U. S. Senator George Wharton Pepper, who had been appointed to Penrose's old seat. Gov. Gifford Pinchot made it a three-way race. Joseph R. Grundy, the Bucks County boss and the most powerful Republican in Pennsylvania, backed Pepper. Vare won narrowly over Pepper, with Pinchot finishing third. Vare defeated the Democratic candidate, William B. Wilson in November—but the U. S. Senate created a special committee to investigate allegations that Vare had spent extraordinarily large sums to win the primary victory. He was denied the seat despite findings of the committee which indicated that only half as much had been spent for him as for Pepper. Joe Grundy was appointed to the Senate seat that Vare had won but could not occupy. (Inquirer)

PHILADELPHIA'S ALAMO is a name often given to old Fort Mifflin, shown here in 1929 when it had a deserted look, for good reason; it was being used as an ammunition depot by the U. S. Navy and was under tight security. The heroic story of the fort began in September of 1777 when the British were advancing on Philadelphia. The city fell, but the 400 Americans in the fort refused to surrender. Located on the Delaware River downstream from the mouth of the Schuylkill, in what is now Southwest Philadelphia, the fort was several miles from the city at that time. For seven weeks the tiny band of defenders held off 12,000 British troops and a British fleet with 250 guns which fired on the fort day after day. Finally, after it had been pounded to pieces, the British stormed in. Only forty men had survived the onslaught. The fort was rebuilt in 1798 and, after long military service, is now open to the public as a memorial to the men who fought and died there in that bleak autumn of 1777, when it seemed to so many in Philadelphia and elsewhere that the struggle for independence was certain to fail. (Inquirer)

ROBIN HOOD DELL opens its 1931 season with a concert by the Philadelphia Orchestra. The amphitheater in Fairmount Park was built in 1930. Many trees originally left standing were later cut down, amid controversy between nature lovers and music lovers, to provide a better view. (Inquirer)

LEOPOLD STOKOWSKI, conductor of the Philadelphia Orchestra from 1912 to 1936, directed an aggregation of unemployed musicians on Reyburn Plaza in 1932 during the depths of the Depression. The group later gave a benefit concert in Convention Hall, with proceeds going to musicians in financial need. It was Stokowski, a colorful figure both on and off the podium, who developed the Philadelphia Orchestra, founded in 1900, into what many critics believe was, and still is, the best orchestra in the world. (Inquirer)

THE WALTON on the southeast corner of Broad and Locust streets was one of the city's finest hotels when this photograph was taken in 1936. Located across the street from the Academy of Music, it also was a center of Philadelphia night life, featuring some of the nation's top entertainers and dance bands. In back of the Walton, on Locust Street, was the Sylvania—another outstanding hotel with a super-elegant lobby and a dining room to match. The Walton was torn down to make way for a parking lot. The Sylvania, still standing, was converted into an apartment house. (Inquirer)

WILLIE SUTTON, the notorius bank robber and prison-escape artist who was known as Slick Willie, made this branch of the old Corn Exchange National Bank on the southwest corner of 60th and Ludlow streets famous when he robbed it of $10,000 in 1934. That was big money in those days. Sentenced to twenty-five to fifty years, he made a career of ingenious escapes and attempted escapes from Philadelphia prisons. (Inquirer)

NOMINATED for a second term at the 1936 Democratic National Convention held in Convention Hall, President Franklin D. Roosevelt waves to a crowd of 100,000 at Franklin Field after giving his acceptance speech. Senator Joseph T. Robinson of Arkansas, the convention chairman, is at the left; next to him is Vice President John Nance Garner, also nominated for a second term. On the other side of the President is his eldest son, James, and Democratic National Chairman James A. Farley is on the right. (Inquirer)

195

FATHER DIVINE was a fabulously successful Philadelphia evangelist and the spiritual leader of thousands of devoted followers. He was photographed in 1939 in a car outside Broad Street Station with his first wife, Peninah, the first Mother Divine. (Inquirer)

THE FIRST ARMY-NAVY GAME at Municipal Stadium was held in 1936 with 102,000 looking on. This photograph shows Midshipmen on parade before the game, which Navy won 7-0. It was the first over-100,000 crowd to see an Army-Navy game, which previously had been held at Franklin Field for eighteen years. Sellout crowds of 102,000 subsequently became commonplace for the annual inter-service football classic. Philadelphia, selected as the ideal neutral site for the games, is about equidistant from West Point and Annapolis. (Inquirer)

MUMMERS PARADES up Broad Street on New Year's Day became increasingly attractive in costumes and decorative displays over the years. Shown in the 1939 parade is the Lobster Club, which won first prize in the fancy dress division. (Inquirer)

EMPTY SEATS on the top level of this south-bound Broad Street bus, making the turn around City Hall in 1939, were typical during non-rush hours. Although the top deck offered a superior view, most regular riders stayed below when they could get seats there. Climbing or descending the spiral stairs at the rear of a moving bus was not for the feeble or the faint-hearted. Broad Street, which extends twelve miles within the city limits, is still said to be the longest straight street in the world—but unless you're walking, don't try to keep going straight when you reach City Hall. (Inquirer)

CIGARETTE SMOKING by women became both popular and fashionable during the 1930s, along with hats tilted at rakish angles. This photograph was taken in 1939 at the Academy of Music, during intermission at the first concert of the season by the Philadelphia Orchestra. (Inquirer)

JOHN B. KELLY, SR., had become a million-aire by 1940 as head of the nation's largest con-tracting firm specializing in brickwork. "Kelly for Brickwork" was his slogan. But twenty years earlier, as the world's foremost rower, he had not been allowed to compete for the Diamond Sculls at the Henley Regatta in England be-cause, it was declared, as a former bricklayer he was ineligible under a rule prohibiting partici-pation in the race by anyone who had "worked with his hands." Later that same year, 1920, he won two Olympic gold medals sculling at Antwerp, in the singles and doubles, teamed with Paul V. Costello in the latter event. In the 1924 Olympics at Paris they won again in the doubles. Kelly was Democratic nominee for mayor in 1935 and, although he lost that elec-tion, became a key figure in the reform move-ment that brought the Democratic Party to power in City Hall in the 1950s under a new City Charter. He was the father of Grace Kelly, who became the Princess of Monaco. (Inquirer)

A GIANT COCKTAIL is made by the stadium clean-up crew pouring remnants of whisky bottles into a jug after the 1939 Army-Navy game. There's no use letting it go to waste. A good time was had by all. (Inquirer)

DOWN MEMORY LANE was a journey not so grand in 1940 for this elderly couple who had worked twenty-eight years at Nixon's Grand Opera House at Broad Street and Montgomery Avenue. As they were looking through the scrapbook they had kept all those years, telling about the hundreds of actors and actresses who had appeared at Nixon's, the wreckers were preparing to tear the old theatre down. The Depression and competition from the movies combined to kill live entertainment in all but a handful of Philadelphia theatres. (Inquirer)

CARPENTERS' HALL, on the south side of Chestnut Street east of Fourth, had been hemmed in for many years by other buildings. It became visible from Fourth Street in 1941 when the old Forrest Building was torn down. The First Continental Congress met in Carpenters' Hall in 1774 as the city and a nation not yet born moved deeper into crisis that would lead to war for independence. When this photograph was taken, the city and the nation soon would be tested by crisis and war again, as secret plans were being made half a world away for an attack that would live in infamy—at a place called Pearl Harbor. (Inquirer)

EUGENE ORMANDY, who succeeded Stokowski as conductor of the Philadelphia Orchestra in 1936, handles the baton at the first rehearsal for the 1940-41 season. Stokowski had brought the music of the great orchestra to vast new audiences through recordings and radio broadcasting, and Ormandy continued the trend through the use of television and the airplane. He put the orchestra on the road—or, more precisely, in the air—to the delight of audiences in countries all over the world, including the Soviet Union and China. (Inquirer)

THE REPUBLICAN NATIONAL CONVENTION of 1940 proved that a dark-horse candidate with no political experience could win the Presidential nomination, with the help of a vocal and persistent cheering section in the gallery. Thomas E. Dewey, shown at a pre-convention press conference on June 22 in his headquarters at the Walton Hotel *(top, facing page)*, had strong delegate support. The New York racket-buster, as a special prosecutor investigating organized crime, had obtained seventy-two convictions against underworld figures. But six days after a confident Dewey had held that press conference, Wendell L. Willkie *(right)* broke into a smile at his headquarters in the Benjamin Franklin Hotel when he heard on the radio that he had been nominated on the sixth ballot. The interior view of Convention Hall *(below)* includes part of the press section in the foreground. Rep. Joseph W. Martin of Massachusetts, at the right in the group on the rostrum, is supervising the roll call of the states during the Presidential balloting. Martin, minority leader in the House of Representatives, was the convention chairman. Throughout the roll calls, the thunderous chant from the balcony, repeated over and over, kept getting stronger: "We want Willkie." They finally got Willkie. (Inquirer)

CAMPAIGNING in South Philadelphia in 1940, seeking an unprecedented third term, President Roosevelt stopped outside the U. S. Naval Hospital to shake hands with a patient. (Inquirer)

OLD SWEDES' CHURCH early in 1942 *(below)* was a picture of peace and stability in a world at war. Located at Swanson and Christian streets in the Southwark section of South Philadelphia originally settled by the Swedes, it was completed in 1700 and is the oldest church in the city. Episcopal services are still held there. (Inquirer)

War, Reform, Renaissance: 1942 to Early 1950s

WORLD WAR II, while calling many Philadelphians to far-flung battlefields and creating acute shortages in consumer goods on the home front, did not have a negative effect on the city's economy. To the contrary, there were generally more jobs than people available to fill them. As a seaport, as a railroad center, as a great industrial city, as the locale of numerous military installations including a giant Navy Yard, Philadelphia became a war-time boom town. Military and civilian personnel were at work around the clock producing and moving goods for the war effort. There was anguish as the casualty lists grew, but they spurred people to even greater effort. The commitment to victory was intense. Confidence in the outcome never faltered. The only question was how long it would take.

With jobs to be had, there was an influx of people to take them. Much of the migration was from small towns and rural areas. Much of it was from the South. Much of it was black.

After the war there was a momentary letdown in the economy, but only until the transition could be made from producing the goods of war to fulfilling pent-up demands for all the things unobtainable during the war. Migration into the city continued, and the migration from the city to the suburbs resumed. The outward migration escalated rapidly in the late 1940s and was nearly all white.

The downward slide in population during the 1930s was reversed in the 1940s. Philadelphia passed the two-million mark in the 1950 census—with 2,071,000 inhabitants. There was a gain of 140,000 in population during the decade, and 126,000 of that gain was black. In 1950, blacks comprised 18 percent of the city's population. That percentage would increase to 26 in

1960 and 34 in 1970. There was a loss in population during the 1950s and 1960s, but in both decades the black population increased. In the 1950s, it increased 153,000, the largest black gain in the city's history. As mentioned in a previous chapter, Philadelphia had approximately the same population in 1970 that it had in 1930–1,950,000–but during that forty-year span there was a decline of 448,000 in the white population and an increase of 434,000 in the black population. The other races, principally Puerto Rican, increased from 2,000 to 16,000 during those four decades.

In the Far Northeast, a section of the city that was mostly open country before the war, a tremendous building boom began in the late 1940s and continued in the decades that followed. Virtually no new housing was built during the war. The post-war marriage and baby boom sent housing demand soaring. Open space for new homes was in the Northeast and in the suburbs— and that is where the houses were built. The Philadelphia Metropolitan Area grew rapidly in population, and soon there would be more people living in the suburbs than in the city. By 1970, the metropolitan area would have 4,824,000 inhabitants, with 2,874,000 of them in the suburbs.

But the city's development was not confined to the Northeast. A Home Rule Charter was approved by the voters on April 17, 1951, as the culmination of the reform movement. It reduced the size of the City Council from 22 to 17 and greatly strengthened the powers of the mayor. In November of that year, Democrats won their first mayoral election in seventy years. Thus in January of 1952, when the new Charter took effect, there was a new party in power. And it was in the 1950s that revitalization of center-city began in earnest—with new office buildings and apartment houses west of City Hall

TRACTOR-TRAILERS had begun to complicate traffic problems on Philadelphia streets before the war and would replace conventional trucks in large numbers when postwar production returned to normal. The view is to the south in this 1942 photograph of the old wholesale produce market on Dock Street. One tractor-trailer driver had parked his rig in the jack-knife position, which left more space in the middle of the street but reduced the vehicle capacity of the loading platforms. Tractor-trailers, which could not park bumper-to-bumper in opposite sides of Dock Street without blocking traffic, contributed to the abandonment of the market. It was replaced in 1959 by the spacious, 388-acre Food Distribution Center on Pattison Avenue, which was the world's first industrial park devoted exclusively to food. (Inquirer)

and on the Parkway, massive renovation and restoration in the Independence Hall area, and a general upgrading of centrally located residential areas, most notably in Society Hill.

The Philadelphia story of post-war progress, blending the old with the new, the modern with the historic, the commercial with the cultural, the efficient with the esthetic, is an unfinished story. The middle of the twentieth century was in many ways a turning point. It marked the end of yesterday's Philadelphia and the beginning of today's—and tomorrow's.

OPEN-AIR TROLLEYS in Fairmount Park *(below),* running in two-car trains to accommodate the crowds, did a brisk business during the war with gasoline and tire shortages keeping people, those not in the military, close to home. Woodside Amusement Park was the most popular trolley stop. Drive-it-yourself water skooters *(right)* still had fuel early in 1942 and were a major attraction for the younger set. (Inquirer)

THE OLDEST STREET in the United States with its original homes still occupied, Elfreth's Alley held its annual open house in 1942 despite the war and drew a large crowd seeking relief from the battlefront news, which was at that time nearly all bad. Many of the residences were built in the early 1700s. The one-block-long alley near the waterfront north of Arch Street is named after a blacksmith who was an early resident, Jeremiah Elfreth. (Inquirer)

WAR-TIME SHORTAGES of gasoline and tires, especially the latter, required extraordinary conservation measures by the Philadelphia Transportation Company even though it had priority access to limited supplies. When not in use during off-peak hours, buses were parked in the nearest available space at the end of their runs *(above)* rather than returned to PTC garages. These double-deckers used on Broad Street routes were lined up near Municipal Stadium in September of 1942. But by December many single-deck buses, such as the ones shown on blocks in a lot at 15th and Huntingdon streets *(below)*, were out of service because their tires had worn out and no replacements could be obtained. Double-deckers, because they consumed less fuel and fewer tires on a passenger-mile basis, had first call on available supplies. (Inquirer)

CRAMP SHIPYARD in Kensington, which had been idle for years after World War I, was back in operation at full capacity in World War II, but as these 1943 photographs show, it wasn't all work. Volunteer musicians and dancers *(above)* entertained the workers regularly in what came to be known as the Lunch Time Follies, and show girls from Philadelphia night spots, which flourished during the war, did their bit for Uncle Sam at lunch-time War Bond rallies *(below)*. Each bond purchased by a shipyard worker entitled him to a dance with the girl of his choice. Sales were brisk. (Inquirer)

STAND-SIT SEATS were introduced in 1943 to increase trolley car seating capacity twenty percent as the wartime gasoline and tire shortages grew worse. Trolleys had to bear increasing responsibility for getting workers to and from defense industries and military installations. Passengers were in a half-sitting, half-standing position. (Inquirer)

WOMEN had a major role in defense work during the war. Security was tight but in 1943, for the first time since Pearl Harbor, the War Department permitted the release of photographs taken inside Frankford Arsenal. This woman was operating a machine that stamped heads on cartridge cases. (Inquirer)

THE CONGRESSIONAL LIMITED, en route from Washington to New York, derailed on a curve at Frankford Junction in North Philadelphia on September 5, 1943, killing eighty people and injuring one hundred and twenty-nine. Cars piled up like match sticks after crashing into a steel tower supporting overhead power lines. The Pennsylvania Railroad's north-south passenger service through Philadelphia had been electrified since 1933. Despite some tragic train wrecks, the railroads performed heroic service during the war—bearing the brunt of both freight and passenger transport, including troop movements. (Inquirer)

WALTER ANNENBERG, then publisher of *The Inquirer*, assists a daughter, Wallis, in an unveiling ceremony at Strawbridge and Clothier in 1943 during the department store's seventy-fifth anniversary celebration. The plaque is a reprint of an *Inquirer* editorial. A quarter-century later, Annenberg became U. S. ambassador to Great Britain and subsequently sold *The Inquirer* and *The Daily News* to Knight Newspapers. He also disposed of television and radio stations in Philadelphia and other cities, but retained some elements of his publishing empire—including *TV Guide, The Racing Form,* and *Seventeen* magazine. (Inquirer)

MARIAN ANDERSON at age thirty-six in 1944 already was a world-renowned contralto starring on nationwide network radio shows. Eleven years later, the Philadelphia native and graduate of South Philadelphia High School would become the first black ever to sing with the New York Metropolitan Opera Company. (Inquirer)

THE FIRST BLACK MOTORMAN on a Philadelphia trolley, Thomas E. Allen, receives operating instructions from William Poisel on the Philadelphia Transportation Company tracks at Third Street and Wyoming Avenue in 1944. The breakthrough for equal employment opportunity came during the wartime shortage of manpower on the home front. Unfortunately, even under these circumstances, progress against racial discrimination did not come easily. It was accompanied by a strike and violence, but Pennsylvania National Guardsmen in full combat gear got the trolleys through. (Inquirer)

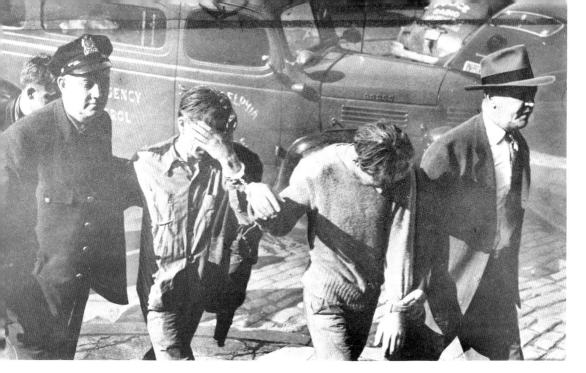

COVERING HIS FACE, bankrobber Willie Sutton was embarrassed by his early recapture on North 24th Street soon after he and four other convicts had tunneled their way out of Eastern State Penitentiary in 1945. All were caught quickly. This was Sutton's fifth escape attempt from Eastern Pen. After a later escape from Holmesburg Prison in Northeast Philadelphia, he was at large for five years. His successful escapes included one from Sing Sing in New York. (Inquirer)

A VICTORY KISS for her young son in Independence Square, after telling him that Daddy would be home soon, was this woman's way of celebrating the end of the war in Europe on May 7, 1945. Germany's unconditional surrender was signed that day but the official cessation of hostilities was on May 8, Philadelphia time. Thus, the latter date came to be celebrated in later years as V-E Day. (Inquirer)

V-J DAY celebrations on August 14, 1945, started early for many, including this couple in City Hall Courtyard *(below)*, as word of impending peace swept through the city. (Inquirer)

THIS ISN'T DETROIT–it's the Budd Company in Philadelphia, where a giant press stamped out auto bodies in 1946 as this firm and other industries made the transition from wartime to peacetime production. (Free Library)

THE FIRST POSTWAR EASTER in 1946 brought buyers to stores in droves seeking items that had not been available for years. Bunnies went over big at Gimbels. (Inquirer)

AFTER THE WAR, Philadelphians were anxious to put their minds to other things—like warfare on ever. Navy won, 14-7. (Inquirer)

the gridiron at Franklin Field. This October afternoon in 1945 was not a happy one for Penn, how-

SWEET ANGEL was the name Father Divine, then a widower, gave to his second wife, Edna Rose Ritchings, when they were married in 1946. She was more formally known as Mother Divine. (Inquirer)

FOUR FERRYBOATS between Philadelphia and Camden were still in operation in 1946. In the background, to the left of this ferry, is the old Wilson Line Pier with one of the line's excursion boats tied up there. The Wilson Line river cruises included daytime sightseeing trips and moonlight voyages with a dance band aboard. Some of the boats stopped at Riverview Beach at Pennsville, New Jersey, where an amusement park was a popular attraction. (Inquirer)

WOODSIDE PARK had three roller coasters—one for the timid, one for the adventurous, and one called the Wildcat *(right)* for the very, very brave. Its almost vertical drops and hairpin curves provided unforgettable thrills for those who had the courage to try them. For the smaller fry, the Baby Whip *(below)* was frightening for some, while others just accepted it philosophically. For generations of Philadelphians, the joys and challenges of Woodside rides were as much a part of growing up as double-decker buses and picnics in the park. These pictures were taken in 1946. A decade later, Woodside Park closed its gates and was torn down. It had been built in the Gay Nineties and couldn't make it in the Fast Fifties. (Inquirer)

AFTER FIFTY YEARS of clickety-clacking through woods and meadow, the Fairmount Park trolleys died in 1946. The last runs were on September 9. With the end of the war came the end of gasoline and tire shortages, and new cars were rolling off assembly lines. A trolley ride in the park was too tame for people who had done without to win the war and now wanted to live it up. These photographs were taken during the trolleys' last days. At the top, a conductor rides on the running board. Benches were the width of the car, with no center aisles, and conductors walked along the running boards to collect tickets. At the bottom, a trolley heads for the barns near West River Drive; it was the end of an era, the end of a slower and simpler life. Before another fifteen years would pass, the Schuylkill Expressway would be blasted and bulldozed through the park, bringing to sylvan surroundings the roar of cars and trucks, bumper to bumper, fender to fender. (Inquirer)

THE PHILADELPHIA EAGLES were flying high in more ways than one after the war. The team travel-
ed to Los Angeles by chartered plane for the 1946 season opener against the Rams. En route, Coach
Greasy Neale reviewed films of the 1945 Eagles-Rams game at Shibe Park; they had been the Cleveland
Rams that year. Coach Neale guided the Eagles to National Football League championships in 1948 and
1949 with halfback Steve Van Buren, one of football's all-time great runners, as the star of the team.
Tommy Thompson was the quarterback. (Inquirer)

STRING BANDS that greet each New Year with toe-tapping music as they march up Broad Street in the
annual Mummers Parade began providing a bonus of musical enjoyment with mid-winter indoor shows
at Convention Hall. This is the Ferko String Band performing in 1947. It had won first prize in the New
Year's parade that year, and band leader Joe Ferko was celebrating his silver anniversary with the organization. (Inquirer)

SNOW SPELLS TROUBLE for some people but it has meant fun for every young generation—such as these sledders on Flat Iron Hill in Fairmount Park in 1948. The 2601 Parkway apartment house is in the background. It looks a bit chilly, but the coldest day on record in Philadelphia was February 9, 1934, when the temperature dropped to eleven degrees below zero. (Inquirer)

[136]

MINOR LEAGUE HOCKEY was played at the Philadelphia Arena at 46th and Market streets for many years before the Spectrum was built on South Broad Street in 1967, and the Flyers were organized to represent the city in the National Hockey League. The 1949 photograph at the Arena was taken during the playing of the National Anthem before a game between the old Philadelphia Rockets and Hershey. The Philadelphia team was later known as the Ramblers. The Arena, which seated a little over 5,000 for hockey games, opened in 1920 and was originally called the Philadelphia Auditorium and Ice Palace. (Inquirer)

GRACE KELLY at age seventeen in 1947 may have been the prettiest girl in Philadelphia. With talent to match her beauty, she was a Hollywood star at twenty and won an Academy Award before her storybook romance and wedding that made her the Princess of Monaco. (Inquirer)

THE FRANKLIN INSTITUTE, founded in 1824 and located on Logan Square since 1934, is the scene of annual memorial services on Benjamin Franklin's birthday, January 17. Speaking on that occasion in front of the Franklin statue in 1947 was Gov. John C. Bell, Jr., a Philadelphian who was governor for just nineteen days—from January 2 to 21, 1947. He had been lieutenant governor and had moved up when Gov. Edward Martin resigned, shortly before the end of his term, to take his seat in the U. S. Senate, for which he had been elected the previous November. Bell, who later became chief justice of the Pennsylvania Supreme Court, was one of the nation's leading tennis players in the 1920s and early 1930s. The Franklin Institute, primarily a science museum and a scientific research and testing organization, is a memorial to Franklin and houses an extensive historical exhibit honoring the greatest Philadelphian. (Inquirer)

HAROLD E. STASSEN, who as governor of Minnesota had delivered the keynote address at the 1940 Republican National Convention in Philadelphia and had been floor manager for Wendell Willkie in his successful bid for the nomination, returned to the scene of that triumph in 1948 as a candidate for the nomination himself. Again the man to beat was Thomas E. Dewey, who had been elected governor of New York and had won the GOP nomination for President in 1944. These photographs show the floor demonstrations for each candidate as their names were placed in nomination at Convention Hall. Although he couldn't stop Dewey this time, Stassen took a liking to Philadelphia and made it his home. He was president of the University of Pennsylvania for five years and, subsequently, as the Republican nominee, an unsuccessful candidate for mayor. (Inquirer)

PRESIDENT HARRY S. TRUMAN was nominated to run for a full term at the 1948 Democratic National Convention in Philadelphia. This was the scene in Convention Hall during the floor demonstration by Truman supporters. Three months later, in October, President Truman was campaigning in Philadelphia and visited the Richard Allen Homes project at 12th and Parrish streets. Riding beside the President in the open car was Maurice Osser, a Democratic candidate for Congress. More than a quarter of a century after this photo was taken, Osser went to jail after a conviction on charges of misusing his office as a city commissioner to extract payoff from a company providing ballots for the city. (Inquirer)

FRESH FROM VICTORY in the November election, President Truman attended the 1948 Army-Navy game with Mrs. Truman and their daughter Margaret. He held up a megaphone before the kickoff to let it be known that he would be doing plenty of cheering, and he wished good luck to the service academy commandants, Major General Maxwell D. Taylor and Rear Admiral James C. Holloway. Taylor, who had a brilliant combat record in Europe during World War II, could not have guessed on that pleasant day in Municipal Stadium that he would have tough and frustrating assignments in two more wars—Korea and Vietnam. (Inquirer)

JERSEY JOE WALCOTT had a chat with Harry Truman when the President, while campaigning in the Philadelphia area, went across the river to Camden. Walcott still holds the record as the oldest man ever to win the heavyweight championship. He was thirty-seven when he took the title from Ezzard Charles with a seventh-round knockout at Pittsburgh in 1951. Jersey Joe lost the title the following year in a memorable fight in Philadelphia's Municipal Stadium, when Rocky Marciano knocked him out in the thirteenth round. (Inquirer)

CHUCK BEDNARIK, widely recognized as the greatest center in the history of football, received a proud handshake from coach George Munger at the University of Pennsylvania's annual football dinner after the 1948 season. For the Penn All-American, his college playing days were over, but an even more brilliant pro career was about to begin. For Penn, an era was ending. The Bednarik years were "the last hurrah" for the Quakers as a national football power. The sport was de-emphasized, and crowds diminished accordingly. Principal beneficiaries were the Philadelphia Eagles. As fans lost interest in Penn, they turned to the pros.

People who had rooted for Bednarik at Penn, continued to root for him as the first-round draft pick of the Eagles. Remarkably fast and agile for a 235-pound lineman, Bednarik played center on offense and linebacker on defense throughout his career, though platoon football had become the standard. (Inquirer)

RICHARDSON DILWORTH, right, shakes hands with Sheriff Austin Meehan before their celebrated debate at the Academy of Music in 1949. A full house heard Meehan, the city's Republican leader, and Dilworth, the fiery orator of the Democratic reform movement, exchange bitter verbal volleys laced with charges and countercharges. It was a turning point in Philadelphia political history. The fact that Meehan even condescended to debate Dilworth signified that the Republicans were in trouble. Two years later, the voters adopted a new City Charter and elected Joseph S. Clark, Jr., another reform leader, as mayor and Dilworth district attorney, ending Republican control of City Hall that had extended back to the 1880s. Dilworth was twice elected mayor, and was twice the Democratic nominee for governor but failed to get elected. He capped a long and distinguished career of public service as president of the Board of Education. (Inquirer)

THOMAS EAKINS, the famous Philadelphia painter, would have approved of this 1949 class at the Pennsylvania Academy of the Fine Arts. Eakins, who had been a student at the Academy and later became its director, resigned under fire in a memorable controversy in 1886, when he shocked some Philadelphians by employing a nude male model for a woman's art class. (Inquirer)

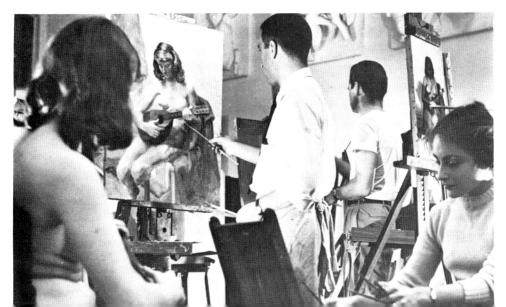

A SILENT CRITIC was unimpressed by the work on display at an art exhibit in Rittenhouse Square. The overcoated gentleman dozed off on his favorite bench. Annual clothesline art exhibits on the square had achieved great popularity by the early 1950s, but the enthusiasm was obviously not unanimous. (Free Library)

THE REV. LEON H. SULLIVAN *(right)* was twenty-eight years old when he arrived in Philadelphia in 1950 to become pastor of Zion Baptist Church. In the decades ahead he would achieve nationwide renown for his pioneering job training and motivation development programs for the unskilled of all races. As founder of Opportunities Industrialization Centers in Philadelphia, he provided spectacular proof that disadvantaged persons previously thought unemployable or only marginally employable could be transformed into productive and dependable workers. Dr. Sullivan also gave leadership and inspiration to successful ventures in black capitalism, including retail shopping facilities and industrial plants managed and owned by blacks. He was the first black to become a member of the board of directors of the General Motors Corporation. (Inquirer)

[142]

PEARL BAILEY in her early thirties had become a nationally acclaimed singing star by 1950. The multi-talented Philadelphian would achieve even greater stardom in the theater, in motion pictures, and on television not only as a singer, but as a comedienne, actress, and homespun philosopher. (Inquirer)

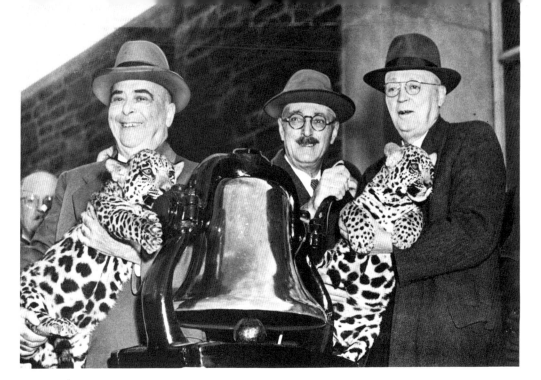

AMERICA'S FIRST ZOO, the Philadelphia Zoological Garden, was opened in 1874 and embarked on a major modernization program in 1951 with the opening of a new building for lions, tigers, and other carnivores, featuring outdoor landscaped areas enclosed by moats instead of bars. Opening ceremonies included a bit of horseplay—or was it catplay? Mayor Bernard Samuel (left) and William Cadwalader, president of the Zoological Society of Philadelphia, held twin jaguar cubs while Joseph Carson, president of the Fairmount Park Commission, rang the dinner bell signaling the first mealtime for the animals in their new home. (Inquirer)

THE AUTOMAT was invented in Philadelphia. Horn & Hardart opened the world's first in 1902 on the south side of Chestnut Street west of Eighth. These two young people were at the grand opening of a Horn & Hardart Automat in Reading Terminal in 1950. For dessert, one chose apple pie and the other lemon meringue—each at a price of three nickels. Automats for more than half a century were considered the ultimate in fast food service. Customers looked at the available choices through glass doors. When coins were put in the slot and the handle turned, the door opened and the customer helped himself. Workers on the other side replenished each cubicle as it was emptied. Revolutionary improvements in fast food operations pioneered by hamburger chains made the Automats cumbersome by comparison. Horn & Hardart closed its last Philadelphia Automat in 1969—the same one that had opened in 1902. During the first half of the twentieth century, Horn & Hardart established full-service restaurants in neighborhoods all over the city. They enjoyed great popularity among families that wanted to eat out at reasonable prices within walking distance of their homes. During the depths of the Depression an occasional dinner at H&H was a memorable treat. (Inquirer)

ROWING REGATTAS on the Schuylkill have perennially drawn large numbers of spectators. These shells were approaching the finish line in the 1951 Adams Cup Regatta. The Harvard crew won, with Navy second, and Penn third. (Free Library)

THE OLDEST PART of Philadelphia is in this 1951 photograph. The Dock Street Market is in the center, where Dock Creek used to flow and where William Penn landed in 1682. In the distance is Southwark, where the Swedes had settled before Penn's arrival. Maritime activity on the waterfront continues to play a major role in the city's economy, as it has since earliest times. (Inquirer)

INDEPENDENCE MALL was moving from dream to reality in 1952 when this model was unveiled. Seated are Roy F. Larson (left), the architect, and State Secretary of Forests and Waters, Samuel Lewis. Standing are Judge Edwin O. Lewis (left) and Arthur C. Kaufmann. Judge Lewis, as principal founder and first president of the Independence Hall Association, was the prime mover and shaker in the creation of Independence National Historical Park and in the tearing down of blocks of unsightly old buildings in front of Independence Hall so that the area could be transformed into a beautiful mall. It was the vision and persistence of Judge Lewis, more than any other individual, which rescued the birthplace of American independence and the nation's most historic square mile from desecrating urban blight. Kaufmann, as chairman of the Independence National Historical Park Advisory Commission, provided much of the leadership and inspiration to carry on the work begun by Judge Lewis. (Inquirer)

AFTER 264 YEARS, beginning in 1688, ferry service between Philadelphia and New Jersey ended on March 31, 1952. This was one of the last runs on the last day, with the Delaware River Bridge in the background. Ferry customers declined steadily after the bridge opened in 1926. The decline accelerated in 1936 when the Delaware River Bridge Speed Line began rail transit service between Philadelphia and Camden. The Speed Line was a predecessor to the Lindenwold High-Speed Line that went into operation in 1969. In 1925, the peak year for the ferries, they carried as many as 100,000 passengers a day with a departure from each side of the river every three minutes during peak periods. The one-way passenger fare on the ferries in 1952 was ten cents. (Inquirer)

[145]

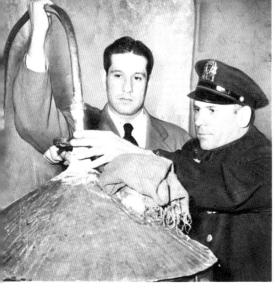

FRANK RIZZO, on the left, was a racket-busting, vice-raiding police captain in 1952. He had advanced rapidly through the ranks, establishing a reputation as a tough, courageous cop. He is helping Patrolman Norman Youngblood put a mash cooker out of operation after a raid on a bootleg liquor ring on North 31st Street. Rizzo later became police commissioner, then mayor. (Inquirer)

THE LAST TRAIN pulled out of Broad Street Station on April 28, 1952. It was an emotional as well as historic moment, ending seventy-one years of service. Eugene Ormandy and the Philadelphia Orchestra were on hand to give a farewell concert, as thousands of Philadelphians came to say goodby. Demolition of the station was ceremonially begun *(left)* by Mayor Joseph S. Clark, Jr., left, and Matthew H. McCloskey, Jr., a prominent builder and Democratic party fund-raiser who later became U. S. ambassador to Ireland. Clark had been mayor only three months. He recognized the occasion as marking the beginning of a spectacular center-city renaissance that would be a highlight of his administration. He later became a U. S. senator. (Inquirer)

DEMOLITION of Broad Street Station had begun in this 1952 photograph. The gingerbread tower on the left is down. So are the roofs over the passenger platforms, revealing how the sixteen tracks fanned into the station and terminated near 15th Street, which tunneled through the station building. To the right of the tracks, extending from 16th to 17th streets on the north side of Filbert Street, is the Pennsylvania Railroad's Suburban Station, later known as Penn Center Station. It was the railroad's only center-city terminal after the demise of Broad Street Station and the Chinese Wall, both of which had been built to stand for centuries. Penn Center rose from the ruins and the towering office buildings, block after block in the heart of the city, were the nation's most spectacular redevelopment of a downtown business area. But the transition symbolized much more: the golden age of railroading was gone. The city that once had the world's largest railroad station and the world's largest locomotive works, only half a mile apart, now had neither. Baldwin had abandoned its locomotive works at Broad and Spring Garden in the 1930s to relocate in suburban Delaware County, but the market for steam locomotives faded swiftly thereafter. (Inquirer)

THE EARLE THEATER on the south side of Market Street east of 11th, was demolished in 1953—a casualty of television and the end of the big band era. Built in 1924, the Earle for many years featured stage shows along with its motion pictures. It was the Philadelphia stop on the big band circuit. Orchestras led by such luminaries as Benny Goodman, Tommy and Jimmy Dorsey, Glenn Miller, Lionel Hampton, Bob Crosby, and Les Brown, and featuring vocalists that included Frank Sinatra and Doris Day—to mention only a few of the dozens of stars in both categories—traveled around the country doing three or four shows a day in movie houses. (Inquirer)

JAMES H. J. TATE was an up-and-coming city councilman in the early 1950s. He would become president of council and then mayor for ten years. He is shown participating in a debate in the council chamber. In the foreground is Councilman Raymond Pace Alexander, a distinguished civil rights leader, who later became a judge. (Inquirer)

TOM GOLA, third from left, was well on his way to becoming a superstar when this photograph was taken on the night of December 21, 1952. The LaSalle College basketball team, unbeaten in eight games, had just returned from California where it had set a new LaSalle scoring record in defeating Stanford 95-80. Left to right are Joe Gilson, Jack French, Gola, Frank O'Hara, Bill Katheder, and Fred Iehle. Gola led LaSalle to a national championship in 1954. His pro career included outstanding years with the old Philadelphia Warriors, predecessors of the 76ers. Gola later became head basketball coach at LaSalle, a state legislator, and city controller. (Inquirer)

JOHN B. KELLY, Jr. *(right),* shown after a rowing workout on the Schuylkill in the early 1950s, wrote a memorable postscript to a notorious chapter in sports history when he won the Diamond Sculls at the Henley Regatta in England in 1947. That was the race from which his famous father had been barred twenty-seven years earlier because he had "worked with his hands" as a bricklayer. Young Kelly won the Diamond Sculls again in 1949. He later became a city councilman. The Princess of Monaco is his sister. (Inquirer)

WILT CHAMBERLAIN *(below)* was a basketball sensation at Overbrook High School in West Philadelphia in the early 1950s. After a brilliant career at the University of Kansas, he returned to Philadelphia as a pro with the old Warriors. He is shown here signing his first contract, with the happy owner of the Warriors, Eddie Gottlieb, pointing to the dotted line. Chamberlain, over seven feet tall, would rewrite the National Basketball Association record book in scoring and rebounding. (Inquirer)

WILLIAM H. HASTIE, pictured in his judicial robes in the 1950s, was the first black ever to serve as a federal court judge anywhere in the United States. He was appointed to the Third Circuit Court of Appeals in Philadelphia by President Truman in 1949. (Inquirer)

THE NEW PASSENGER TERMINAL that cost $15 million was dedicated at International Airport in 1953. Mayor Clark, on the speakers' platform, is raising the flag. The Pan American Strato Clipper, the latest thing in air travel, was open for public inspection. Although the jet age in commercial aviation still was years away, the new airport terminal marked the emergence of the airplane as a major form of public transportation in Philadelphia and a substantial factor in the metropolitan area's economic development. It was significant, and not entirely coincidental, that the new airport terminal was under construction as old Broad Street Station was being torn down. (Inquirer)

INDEPENDENCE MALL construction was about to begin in this 1953 photograph after old buildings on the site had been torn down. For the first time since the eighteenth century could the front facade of America's most historic block be seen in its entirety from a distance at ground level: Independence Hall is in the center; the first-floor windows on the left look into the room where the Declaration of Independence and the Constitution of the United States were adopted in 1776 and 1787, respectively; at left is Old City Hall, where the U. S. Supreme Court held its sessions when Philadelphia was the nation's capital from 1790 to 1800; at right is the Old Capitol of the United States, now known as Congress Hall, where the U. S. Senate and House of Representatives held their sessions from 1790 to 1800. The tall structures on the right, on Sixth Street facing Independence Square, are the Curtis Publishing and *Public Ledger* buildings. The *Saturday Evening Post* and other Curtis magazines were published from the more distant building. The *Public Ledger* and *Evening Ledger* were published in the nearer building. (Inquirer)

THE LIBERTY BELL is Philadelphia's and America's symbolic link with the past and the future. It tolled on July 8, 1776, when the Declaration of Independence, approved in final draft four days earlier by the Second Continental Congress, was given its first public reading to a crowd assembled on Independence Square. It tolled on September 17, 1787, when the Constitution of the United States was adopted by the Federal Constitutional Convention. It was cracked in the early nineteenth century and has become a silent but no less revered voice of liberty. It was cast in 1753, long before the birth of American independence, yet bears the remarkably prophetic inscription from the twenty-fifth chapter of Leviticus: "Proclaim Liberty throughout all the land unto all the inhabitants thereof." In this photograph, taken in the 1950s but conveying a message that is timeless, a young visitor lifts his sister so that she, too, may touch the Liberty Bell and draw inspiration from the unforgettable experience–as millions have done before and millions will do in the years ahead. (Inquirer)

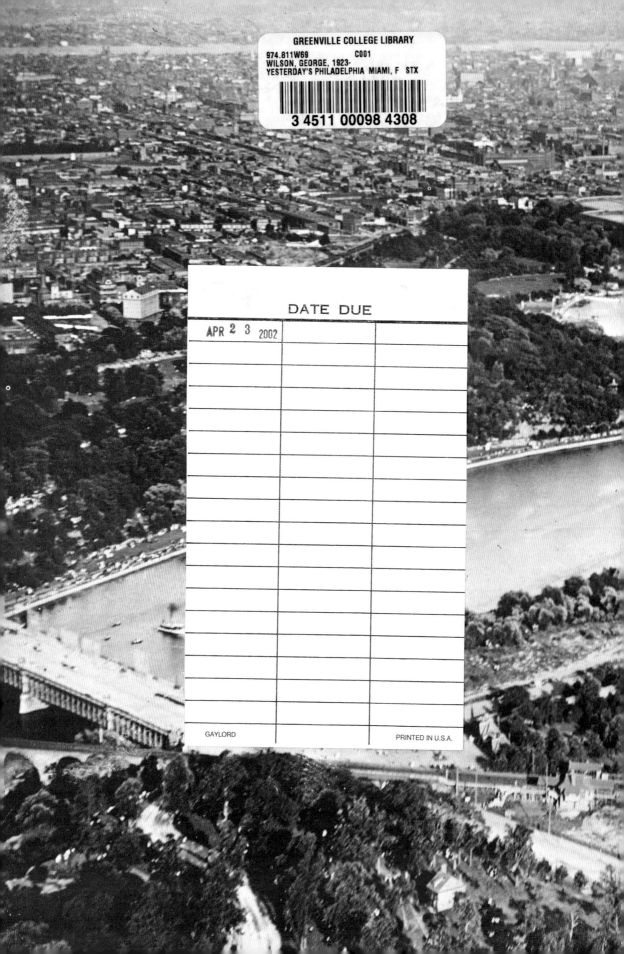

DATE DUE

APR 2 3 2002		
GAYLORD		PRINTED IN U.S.A.